POLICY FOR THE WEST

The world today is divided into three: the Soviet countries, the Western Democracies and those nations not yet committed to either side. Communist 'dynamism' makes it impossible for the relationship between the three to be static. In recent years Communism has made great strides throughout Asia, it is now penetrating into the Middle East and is actively preparing the ground for a further advance in Africa and Latin America.

The present Western policies, Ion Ratiu believes, must inevitably lead to the loss of the uncommitted countries to Communism, and to isolation. He gives the grounds for his belief in a well documented analysis of the international situation.

But he is not a prophet of doom. He urges a re-thinking of Western policies in the conviction that by adapting them to the realities of the world today, and by constructive measures, the Western Democracies can win the ideological struggle, in which their case is stronger than that of any dictatorship of the right or left.

His suggestions are fearlessly honest and eminently practical.

Ion Ratiu is a Rumanian whose family has, for generations, taken an active and prominent part in the affairs of his country. He was in London when Rumania joined the Axis in 1940 and has since remained in England. After studying law and economics he has worked unceasingly to gain knowledge and understanding of his country's problems, particularly in relation to Russia which has now become a world problem.

Recently he has acted as assistant counsel for the defence of the four Rumanian patriots who seized the Soviet Embassy in Berne; and he was responsible for the escape of Opris, the Rumanian Olympic runner who has sought refuge in the West.

Continuous contact with men engaged in international affairs and searching study make his book a contribution which deserves serious consideration.

POLICY

FOR

THE WEST

by

Ion Ratiu

London

THE HARVILL PRESS

Published by
THE HARVILL PRESS LTD.
23 Lower Belgrave Street
London S.W. 1.

1957

Printed in Great Britain by
Wyman & Sons, Ltd., Fakenham

CONTENTS

ACKNOWLEDGEMENTS

My thanks are due to Sally Kay Brass and Jane Cobb whose help has been invaluable.

I. R.

NOTE

Notes (marked * or †) at the end of chapters have been added in view of events which have occurred since the completion of the text.

PART ONE

THE WEST IN PERIL

I

THE PROBLEM

THE communist threat was first recognised quasi-officially, here in the West, about 1947, at the time when George F. Kennan published his now famous article under the pseudonym of 'Mr. X'. The world at large became aware in 1948 that the danger was imminent and that communism might advance unchecked when Czechoslovakia fell under the communist-engineered *coup d'état* that led to Masaryk's dramatic death.

Nearly a decade has passed since then: years punctuated by one communist advance after another. During this time the whole of China, Tibet, North Korea, and North Indo-China, have come under communist rule. This advance would have been even more spectacular had it not been for the bold and correct decisions taken during certain crises by leading Western statesmen. But the advance was only checked at some points of stress by force of arms, and at the cost of the lives of over one hundred thousand young soldiers mobilised by the Western Powers. Given the facts of communist advance in recent years, it is perfectly legitimate to state that, had the true nature of communism been understood, and an effective policy *vis-à-vis* the communist threat applied, the two wars in the Far East need never have taken place. Secondly, we are entitled to ask ourselves: is it right to assume that no further communist advance will be made? Should we not view Khrushchev's and Bulganin's display of vigour during their trips to Yugoslavia, South-East Asia and Great Britain, and the activities of the communist parties in such countries as

3

Indo-China, Malaya or France, to quote only a few examples, as conclusive evidence that, given the opportunity, new areas will be brought under communist control? Once we have answered this question in the affirmative, we must examine the policy which is now pursued by the Western Powers in order to ascertain whether or not this policy is capable (*a*) of meeting the communist challenge, and (*b*) of successfully upholding the cause of liberty in the rest of the world.

II

RED TIDE

THE signs are clear. The immediate objective of world communism, besides consolidating power in the lands already conquered, is to create the favourable conditions which will permit it to make use of its carefully devised and well-tried technique for capturing power, first in Asia and the Middle East, then in Africa, and finally in Latin America and Western Europe. What is the real state of affairs in the non-communist world, and what are the chances of withstanding this 'onward march of communism'? A few examples, taken from each of the broad geographical divisions of the earth, will suffice to indicate the anwer.

Taking Asia first, in Viet Nam, Diem's régime, propped up as it is by American bayonets, has a very tenuous existence—one cold wind from the north, hesitation and lack of resolution on the part of the Western Powers, and it will be swept away.

Afghanistan is in no better position, though not so obviously. The feudal-tribal form of government which obtains there has neither the moral strength nor the material and physical force necessary to withstand successfully a well-directed communist bid for power. The people of Afghanistan would probably rally to the cry of nationalism and follow their leader should their land be invaded. Pride, traditions, and the tenacity of the highlander will certainly serve them in good stead, but they have no arms, and no industrial strength. Moreover, at this moment Afghanistan is of no particular significance to the Western Powers; it is almost isolated from the main stream of international affairs. It would not be surprising, therefore, if Afghanistan were to be among the next victims of communist aggression.

India and Burma have large and vocal communist parties: but the Indians and the Burmese have only just won their freedom from foreign domination. The love and respect which the peoples of these two countries have for their present leaders are such that no mass movement in favour of communism, so long as communism is opposed by them, will make much headway in the immediate future. It can be said that for the time being they are largely immune to communism. In Burma U Nu has stepped down from the Premiership: undoubtedly a concession to pressure from the extreme Left so vocally desirous of closer collaboration with the Soviet Union and Communist China. Yet U Nu, even if in semi-retirement, will exercise a restraining influence. But what will happen when Nehru and U Nu have gone?

Pakistan, though aligned to the West, both through S.E.A.T.O. and M.E.T.O., is now being wooed and courted by the Soviet Union and China.

Thailand is a country with proud traditions. Never in their whole history have the Thai people been subject to foreign rule. Yet the régime there is dictatorial. The people are poor. The pressure of the not far distant lands, newly conquered for communism, is enormous.

Indonesia is a group of scattered islands. No Indonesian Government could hope to achieve any measure of stability unless supported directly, or tolerated, by the large communist force which has made its impact on the people of almost every island in the archipelago.

In the Philippines the communists have been driven underground. The country has close links with the United States and many leaders give their loyal support to Western ideals. But these are still a very small minority. The Government is stable enough. Yet, without United States support, could they hope to ward off the influence of rampant communism on the Asiatic mainland?

Taking the whole of Asia and South-East Asia one can only conclude that the entire area is objectively ripe for communism. There is nothing to stem the tide. Conditions vary from country to country, and certainly, apart from Viet Nam and Afghanistan, and perhaps Laos and Nepal, there is no immediate danger. The communists, in all probability, will embark throughout Asia upon a policy of undermining the confidence of the people in their present rulers, and keep a bold challenge for a later day. Nevertheless, the possibility of a revolution breaking out in any of these countries in the immediate future cannot be ruled out. One should never forget that in no country at present under communist rule were the communists the majority party before they captured power.

The people of South and South-East Asia are largely illiterate. Under the guidance of their present leaders they still refuse to yield power to the communists. But for how long? The people, as distinct from the rulers, have no great love for democracy, even when they understand it.

In fact there are only two factors that today prevent a further spread of communism in Asia: the determination of the Western Powers to hold Asia, and the growing strength of Japan. Japan is not likely to turn communist for a long time to come, but has often been misguided in its policy. Japan is strong by virtue of the industry, self-discipline and self-denial of its people. Yet the increase of population and the needs of the people are so great that sooner or later they will have either to find markets for the produce of their industries, or starve. This means coming into direct contact with communism and communist ideas, for traditionally China is Japan's main market. China may yet again make such overtures, and offer Japan such tempting terms of trade, that the Japanese leaders will not be able to refuse. Where else could they sell? They must trade in the markets which will produce the food they eat, and which they so sorely need. Shigemitzu, the Foreign Secretary, has a decidedly pro-Western attitude. His Premier, Hatoyama, however, advocates a general settlement with the Soviet Union, not hesitating to present himself as favouring close economic co-operation with the communist powers.

The Middle East offers us a different, yet fundamentally similar, picture. Rent and torn by internal jealousies and strife the Arab nations are nevertheless united on one vital point: they want to wipe Israel from the face of the earth. Russia knows this all too well. The Soviet leaders have no particular love for the Arab feudal and capitalist countries. Yet Israel is cast, as it were, in the role of the victim almost by mistake, because by supporting the anti-Israel feeling of the Arabs the Soviets have now entered, and are sure to gain, in the not too distant future, a firm foothold in an area which so far has always been denied to all Russian advances.

The Czechoslovak-Egyptian arms deal dramatised the situation, but the conflict is all too real. In their present mood the Arab leaders, particularly Colonel Nasser, will stop at nothing to gain that arms superiority which they want. All Russia has to do is to accept in exchange for arms such goods as the Arabs are in a position to supply. This they are doing, and it is difficult to see what precise measures, short of war, the West could take to prevent this exchange. Even if it is agreed upon by the Western democracies, a naval blockade is remote from the realm of practical politics. Besides, such a blockade would be in effect an act of war, since ships chartered for the carrying of arms would have to be stopped and their cargoes confiscated. So long as Soviet- or satellite-manufactured arms find their way into the Arab countries the communist penetration in the Middle East is assured; direct contact between various trade delegations will have to be maintained, and a constant inflow of communist technicians into the Arab world, as well as the training of young Arabs in communist countries, will be an absolute necessity. Modern weapons of war cannot be mastered without instruction from highly skilled specialists. And we can be reasonably certain that Moscow will see to it that these technicians will try to impart not only their technical skill but also their political ideas. They will be specially selected and their task will be to spread the communist doctrines.

The whole of the Arab world lives in penury. Colonel Nasser has himself said that the average monthly earnings of an Egyptian amount to about £2. In the other countries of the Middle East the situation is, if anything, worse. Every régime in this area is authoritarian, totalitarian, or outright feudal. The power of the Koran is still great; but so is the power of hunger. If and when the teeming millions of poverty-stricken Arabs, scraping their livelihood out of a barren, unwatered land, are made aware of the communist promise to turn it into a new Garden of Eden, nothing will prevent the formation of a hard core of communist fanatics—if it is not already in existence. The Middle East is the land of fanaticism. In our own day the Middle East has given birth to the Muslim Brotherhood, just as long ago Mohammed was able to carve out for himself a religious empire. In later centuries, one conqueror after another led Islam under the un-furled green banner of the Prophet right across the whole of North Africa into the Iberian peninsula and to the very gates of Vienna. Throughout history one empire after another has sprung up from this area.

That fanaticism is still at work today, as the Western statesmen, who have had direct contact with the present leaders of the Arab world, will bear witness. Some Arab leaders seem to regard the whole broad sweep from the Persian Gulf to the Atlantic Ocean as their own country. This fanaticism could be—and, if no far-reaching measures are taken soon, will be—harnessed to the communist chariot. The communists have already turned other religions into effective expansionist weapons. They will do so again. Soviet Russia has recently sent an important emissary to the newly created, but still insignificant, Kingdom of Libya. The Soviet mission in Cairo is second in importance only to those appointed to the capitals of the Great Powers. It is, therefore, clear that the Soviets are now laying the foundation of a long-term plan for penetration into the Middle East. The decisive bid may be postponed to the next generation, but no opportunity for advance will be missed. In this broad geographical area of the Middle East the position of the West is just as precarious as in the Far East, if not more so. There is no local force, indigenous to the Middle East, that could be pitted against communism. Here again, it is only the determination of the Western Powers not to abandon this area, so vital to them, that still prevents the Soviets from moving in.

The whole of Africa is in turmoil. The dark continent of yesterday is becoming daily more articulate. The striving for self-respect of the native leaders, often educated in the Universities of the West, is pressing for the independence which will give the people of Africa a measure of that human dignity the right to which is openly proclaimed by the Western Powers. This nascent nationalism, day by day gaining in urgency, is on the move. But what the coloured people of Africa want most, so the communists say, the West will never be able to give them. The Africans want nothing short of equality with the white races. They want to be masters in their own house. They will gladly accept such concessions as their present white rulers are willing to give them. They will extort others. They will fight to the death to gain more, as they have so recently done in Kenya. But their long-term objective is the expulsion of the white population, or the complete acceptance by the white settlers in Africa of a role broadly corresponding with their numerical importance. Out of a total population of 150 million people less than 8 millions are white, a ratio of twenty to one. In the whole of Africa there are hardly any compact white settlements where the white man forms a majority, capable of providing the basis of a 'white' political unit. In other words the ultimate objective of all educated Africans is self-government. Inevitably, they must also want to become the rulers of the white minorities in their midst.

Communist propaganda, powerfully directed at Africa today, aims precisely at making the coloured people believe that only communism can ultimately restore to them those rights and dignities which they enjoyed—even if only in a primitive way—before white colonisation began. The communists point out that the white races cannot under any circumstances surrender their power in Africa. Even the benevolent paternalism of the white races, say the communists, can produce nothing more constructive than impracticable schemes, like 'parallel pyramidal development', which aim to placate the just demands of the coloured people while yet maintaining the overriding power of the white settlers.

The Soviet Embassy in Addis Ababa seems to be the real centre of official communist action in Africa. It has a staff of over eighty people. A remote, backward country, undeveloped economically, with no outlets to the sea, Abysinnia hardly justifies such an important diplomatic effort. But Abyssinia is the one African country that is truly independent, with a long and proud history of independence. From Addis Ababa communist propaganda can turn to its greatest advantage the 'objectively' favourable revolutionary conditions which Moscow seems to believe already obtain throughout Africa. When the 'subjective' conditions are also present the communists will strike. The establishment of diplomatic relations with Liberia and Libya is part of the same preparatory action; and the closing down of Soviet consulates in

B

South Africa, by a Nationalist Government committed to a policy of *Apartheid*, is an example of the fear which Soviet espionage and communist propaganda produce.

There is evidence that throughout Africa more and more people are turning to communism. In Cape Province there is already a very important communist party. The enlightened policy pursued by Great Britain in countries like Nigeria, or the relative economic wellbeing enjoyed by the Africans, for example, in the Belgian Congo, may yet prevent any wholesale acceptance of communism by the African leaders as their only salvation. Yet in French Equatorial Africa it is precisely on the borders of such 'advanced' countries as the Gold Coast or Nigeria, that the communist-led and communist-inspired parties made the greatest gains at the general elections early in 1956.

Taking Africa as a whole, one cannot fail to realise that the inroads which communism now makes upon the allegiance of the coloured African leaders is so great that, without an effective, truly imaginative, newly thought-out policy, the prospects for the future are disastrous from a Western point of view. The next moves of Soviet world strategy are likely to affect South-East Asia. Then the Middle East.* But the day is not very remote when the communist bid for power will become active in Africa, and on the present showing it is probably correct to forecast that, once made, it will find a ready response in the hearts of the African people. The Western Powers have an abiding interest in keeping Africa for the free world, but the African people will turn their freely given loyalty only to those who give them a definite promise for the fulfilment of their aspirations. Communism makes such a promise. That it has no foundation in fact is immaterial. Since it has been made the African people may turn to communism.

The Latin-American, republics from the tip of Tierra del Fuego to the Rio Grande, present an apparently safe front. Below this

façade there is great ferment; we have had a glimpse of it in the
Jagan experiment in British Guiana and in the Arbenz régime of
Guatemala. Since government by the people, for the people,
does not obtain anywhere in Latin America, with the possible
exception of Uruguay, the communists will always find a listen-
ing ear. Brazil and Chile have important and powerful communist parties, even though numerically they may appear insignificant. These two countries, next to Uruguay, are the most
developed in the ways of democratic government. The others
are outright dictatorships. Communism lives underground.
No one knows for certain, apart from the initiates, the exact
strength of communism in these countries; but what is certain
is that the more communism is persecuted, the more it produces
martyrs and the stronger it grows. Those who manage to escape the
wrath of the local dictator's security police acquire greater efficiency in the art of undercover subversion and far greater prestige.

The whole of Latin America is still in the expanding phase of
capitalism. Great fortunes are made, little taxation is levied. The
wellbeing of the people largely remains a pious statement made by
politicians seeking election, or a slogan sporadically blared out by
the marching supporters of the militarist would-be dictator.

The lot of the common people is no one's concern. Trade-
unionism in the Western sense—with the possible exception of Chile where it is largely controlled by communists—
hardly exists. Social welfare schemes, if they can be found at all
in these countries, are usually a dead-letter of the law, used by the
loyal agencies of the governments in power for propaganda
purposes and foreign consumption; occasionally social welfare
depends on the private largesse of some local Croesus, who uses
it as an avenue to political or industrial power. This is the
classic breeding ground of communism as Marx originally saw it.

Moreover, Latin America is not only a country of white colonisers and of the *métisse* population associated with them; it is also

13

the country of the descendants of the great Maya, Aztec and Inca civilisations. These Indians, scattered about central America, mainly in Mexico, Peru and Bolivia, live in dire poverty, hardly touched by modern industrial civilisation. But, wherever industry has raised its belching furnaces, these under-privileged people supply the labour force. So far as it can be established, communism to them is still a very vague idea. But there is no reason why they should remain indefinitely uninfected by it. When that day comes, possibly after Asia, the Middle East and Africa have already been engulfed by communism, the well-trained cadres of the South American communist parties will turn their faith into the guiding star of Latin America's future. Recent history has taught us that ignorance of communism is no weapon against communism. It is not the elaborations of the Marxist doctrine that win communist adherents, but the beautiful picture of a future full of justice and plenty for all.

This, then, seems to be the world-wide strategy of Russian communism today. Isolate the hard core of liberal democracy. Isolate the one power they fear: the United States. Isolate the one political force they respect: liberal democracy as it is practised in the Anglo-Saxon world. When that is done, the time of reckoning will have come for Europe, for there the communists still have the greatest active force outside the communist empire. The communist parties of Europe are not the parties of the under-privileged. They are not the parties of some coloured people seeking the recognition of their rights. The communist parties of Europe form an integral part of the body politic of democracy. Therein lies the danger. They are well versed in the democratic machinery of government and are taking an active part in the working of democracy. Yet their sole aim is to destroy democracy, utterly. They use the privileges conferred by democracy on every individual, but deny the spiritual values which have created democracy. They consider themselves to be the soldiers of a new world.

It may well be that of the odd five million votes constantly cast for communism in France in successive elections, the vast majority merely wish to express their impatience with the ineffectual governments of the centre and the constitutional shortcomings of the Fourth Republic. But even assuming that such optimism is warranted, there remains a terrifying mass of people who now live in France but reject the idea of France as a national state. Their allegiance is owed and given to Moscow alone. They accept Moscow as the guide and supreme arbiter of all policy, the ultimate objective of which is the creation of a workers' state of which France will be a part. That France is ripe to be taken over by the communists no one need doubt.

Not one of the countries in Eastern Europe, now under communist rule, had a communist party at all comparable in strength and numbers with that of France. The well-known French individualism, forged through centuries of intellectual eminence and spiritual leadership of the world, is all too real. We could truly say that France today possesses countless leaders, thoroughly imbued with the spirit of democracy. Yet of the countries which could be listed under the broad category of liberal democracy, France is the weakest link because of her extremely effective, disciplined, Moscow-aligned Communist Party. France has a further weakness, the importance of which has often been underestimated. Metropolitan France includes large segments of North Africa, and other North African territories are so closely connected with France, as members of the French Union, that no appraisal of Western Europe, of which France is such an important part, can be accurate without a discussion of the problems of that troublous area, Algeria, Tunisia, and Morocco. Over one million and a half French settlers live in North Africa; and it is estimated that almost one million Arabs live in France, mostly in the south. The whole of this Arab population is, in varying degrees, committed to the overthrow of French rule. Communism has made deep inroads both in French North Africa and among the Arab population now living in France. This large, discontented, under-privileged population, whose eyes are turned towards the Arab world and on a possible resurgent universal Arab state, will gladly help in the destruction of French democracy because in that they see the opportunity to realise their own national aspirations.

The Communist Party of Italy is almost equally strong. In fact it has won more votes than the Communist Party of France, though from a practical point of view Italy must remain a question-mark for the Moscow leaders. Italy not only possesses a very important, well-trained army of communist militants, it also has an articulate, highly effective Catholic Action movement. After all, the Catholic faith remains the most powerful single religious force against communism today. The communist challenge to the world is a long-term one. Of all Western spiritual forces only the Catholic Church can match that challenge with an objective far more lasting. By the very nature of its world-wide organisation Rome views all human problems *sub specie aeternitatis*.

To achieve any degree of accuracy in assessing the situation in Spain today, one must remember the Spanish revolution of the thirties, when the whole of Spain was torn asunder, one half of it willing to shed its blood under the communist banner or, at any rate, under communist leadership. However much opinion in Spain might have veered away from the Reds in the intervening years, no one who has seen the pitiful dwellings dug into the hillside outside Barcelona, or who is aware of the stirrings below the outwardly calm surface so angrily proved by the student disturbances in the spring of 1956, can reject the conclusion that communism, though underground, must still be a powerful force in Spain.

The Scandinavian and the Low Countries are in a happier position. They are prosperous, their populations contented. They are highly civilised, with social organisations which embrace their nations in all aspects. Since the Second World War, the governments of these countries have consistently pursued an enlightened policy which ensures an equable distribution of wealth, as well as a just return for labour. But even here communist parties exist. Though small, they are vocal, and prepared to capture power the moment democracy can no longer find the means, and will, to survive.

Western Germany is probably more immune to communism than any other country. This is not due to any particular qualities of the German people, many though they are. Germany has not only produced the founder and the high priest of communism, it has also had a very strong Communist Party. But the East-West frontier which splits Germany into two halves has been crossed by millions during the last ten years who seek refuge from communism. On the other hand, Germany's new-found faith in democracy has yet to be proved under stress. West Germany's immunity to communism is due, not so much to her loyalty to the ideals cherished by the truly democratic people of the world, though undoubtedly this loyalty already plays an important part, but rather to the knowledge passed on by its victims from the East that communism in practice produces a totalitarian state which sweeps away any claims of the individual against the all-embracing state. But how reliable is West Germany's stand on the side of the West? The present West German Government leaders are whole-heartedly on the side of the Western Powers. They have proved it beyond any possible doubt. But Dr. Adenauer cannot live for ever, and the conquest of Western Europe is still a distant objective in the over-all communist strategy. The Soviet Union strongly desires Germany in her camp. To achieve that she will make great concessions. The men in the Kremlin know that once

Germany is won over, or at least neutralised, an important step towards world dominion will have been made. Many responsible West German leaders, who genuinely believe in democracy, have advocated and still advocate direct dealing with Moscow in order to achieve German unity. Since the split in the Federal Coalition Government and the departure of Dr. Dehler's Free Democratic Party, the position of Dr. Adenauer has been seriously weakened. Public opinion seems to move in favour of a Russo-German deal, *if unity can be achieved.* The situation is all too understandable, the temptation very great. Bishop Otto Dibelius, the head of the Evangelical Church of Germany, made an important and characteristic statement during his visit to Australia early in 1956. He believes that more and more people in Germany wish to reunify Germany as a loose confederation, the two present halves maintaining their own internal economic and social structures. To achieve this, Dr. Dibelius declared, the German people are quite ready to accept permanent neutrality. Even assuming that this ever-increasing pressure for direct Russo-German dealing is successfully resisted by the present Government, no one can tell what the leaders of tomorrow's Germany will do, when Dr. Adenauer has gone. The ghost of Rapallo still powerfully dominates many an informed German mind.

The countries briefly surveyed are representative of the entire non-communist world. They have been chosen because they happen to hold the attention of the world. The communist threat, however, is just as present in many countries not mentioned here, because the communist challenge is addressed to the whole world. As it advances, communism leaves no islands of liberal democracy, nor of any other non-communist form of government. Outside the communist world, liberal democracy, in its full implication, only exists in the West, where there is a full enjoyment of individual liberty by the entire population. Only in the Anglo-

Saxon world and in Western Europe are there soldiers ready to fight for the defence of their present way of life, and a genuine spiritual force that can be pitted against the communist challenge. Throughout the rest of the non-communist world the adherents of democracy are a small body of men; some only pay lip-service to the democratic ideal, but others actually try to educate their people so that democracy may in time take root in their own lands. But it is a terrible mistake to imagine that democracy commands a massive following in any country outside Europe, the Commonwealth and North America. Were communist armed forces to advance tomorrow into Pakistan, or Thailand, or the Middle East, for example, they might be opposed because a foreign invasion would be resented. But if communists in these same countries were to come to power by internal revolution they would soon be able to establish themselves firmly. They would merely be a new dictatorial régime replacing countless previous dictatorial régimes. In these countries the communist advance is checked merely by the power of Western arms, or rather by the threat that arms would be used by the Western democracies. If one considers the world as a whole, therefore, it is time to say that apart from the Western democratic peoples, it is only the weapons of war wielded by the West and by the United States that stand in the way of further communist advance. Nowhere else, except in the Western democracies, are there vast multitudes ready to fight with courage, determination and faith for their cause, should they ever be attacked.

The communists now rule well over 900 million people. Those countries which can safely be considered as practising democracy total a population of less than 500 million people. The other 1,000 or 1,100 million people can be lumped together as uncommitted nations, which have no special love for democracy, nor any intention to fight in order to preserve it since democracy does not exist in their countries. The democratic ideal is approved by many highly civilized intellectual leaders of the uncommitted nations. As a practical political force, however, it must be considered as non-existent there or, at best, in an embryonic state.†

Footnote from p. 12.

* By August 1956 the infiltration of Chinese Communist troops into the Wa state of north-east Burma reached such alarming proportions that the former Burmese Prime Minister U Nu formally asked Mr. Nehru to use his good offices to obtain the withdrawal of the Chinese troops. Until this is effected the Wa state remains, for all intents and purposes, a communist-controlled area.

The tremendous arms build-up in the Middle East from communist sources —far in excess of Egypt's defensive needs—as revealed during the Suez conflict in November 1956, conclusively proves the authenticity of Soviet intentions as here described.

† On October 23rd, 1956 the students of Budapest clashed with units of the Hungarian political police. The full-scale Hungarian national revolution which followed was crushed in blood by Soviet armour.

On October 29th, 1956 the Israelis began the occupation of the Sinai Peninsula. A few days later the Anglo-French forces entered the conflict with the declared purpose of separating the Egyptians from the Israelis along the line of the Suez Canal. The reaction of world opinion to these fateful events is more than instructive. The West was outraged. Soviet brutality and ruthlessness against a freedom-loving people were generally condemned. But outside the confines of the democratic West the reaction was quite different. The Colombo Powers described Russia's aggression 'a reintroduction of troops'. Mr. Nehru found some justification for it. 'The Soviet intervention was necessary,' said Marshal Tito, because 'it saved socialism in Hungary' . . . Without this intervention 'chaos, civil war, counter-revolution and a new world war' would have followed, added the Yugoslav communist dictator. Mr. Kuznetsov, the U.S.S.R. representative at the United Nations General Assembly, glibly asserted that reaction was crushed in Hungary 'with the self-sacrifice of the Soviet military forces'. From Moscow Bulganin spoke of sending 'volunteers' to repel the 'imperialist aggressors' from the Middle East.

In this deliberately-created false atmosphere the true merits of Hungary's plight, and of Nasser's provocations, were ignored or forgotten. Anglo-French action was condemned at the United Nations by all representatives with the exception of Australia and New Zealand. In fact, on balance, communism emerged from this succession of crises considerably strengthened everywhere in the world except in Western Europe and America. And this loss of ground in the West is of no immediate importance to world communism. For the time being the West is not to be 'liberated', but merely isolated. Great strides are made by communism where it most matters, in Asia and the Middle East—the next objectives.

III

FILLING THE GAPS

THIS is the global picture. The evidence is overwhelming that the over-all communist strategy aims at advancing into South-east Asia and the Middle East, then into Africa and finally into Latin America. Thus, the communists hope to isolate the Western Powers in preparation for the final attack, which will most probably start from within the very organism of the free world. Of course, the Soviets will adapt their plan to the needs of the moment. Should at any time an opportunity arise to advance with impunity they will do so, even if it may not fit perfectly into the pattern. But what the free world tends to ignore is the fact that the whole of the communist method of government is based on detailed, long-term planning—nothing is left to chance.

The avowed policy of the Western Powers is to stop the further spread of communism, so long as communism is not freely chosen by the majority of the people. This has been explicit or implicit in countless statements and commitments. The practical measures by which this policy has so far been put into practice could be listed under several headings.

First, there is the policy of containment, which amounts to warning the Soviet Union that the United States and her allies will use force to prevent the communists from seizing power by force in any area not now under their control. The most important and extreme example of this policy was the war in Korea. It is all too often argued that this war would never have taken place had it been made quite clear to the communists that Korea is of such strategic importance to the Western world that it would come to Korea's defence. This may or may not be correct. The fact remains that Korea provides the test case of the policy of containment. The United States showed its determination to repel by force a communist attempt to capture power by force. In accordance with the policy of containment American military bases have been set up right round the communist world. In this way any communist military action, started from communist territory, can be opposed on the spot.

In view of the vastness of the problem and the enormous length of the frontier within which communism must be contained, the policy of containment only makes sense if it is viewed together with the policy of deterrents. In practice the policy of deterrents amounts to an explicit threat that the democratic world would use, not only an 'unalterable' force to stop aggression, but would also have recourse to those weapons of mass destruction which would make any communist aggression extremely dangerous to the main communist powers themselves. In fact the Western powers are serving notice that communist aggression may lead to retaliation on a far larger scale and with far more comprehensive objectives than the limited front on which the communists are advancing. For some years this policy of deterrents was effective while America had the virtual monopoly of the atom bomb; and, later, by virtue of America's superiority in the development of nuclear weapons. Now, however, the situation is changed, for it is clear that the Russians have equalled, if not overtaken, in some respects at any rate, the American preparedness for nuclear warfare. Under the circumstances the policy of deterrents can only have a meaning if the democratic countries serve notice to Moscow and to Peking that any further advance would lead to a shattering counter-blow directed against the communist centre and aimed at the complete crippling of communist heavy industry, without which they could not fight a modern war.

This important rider has never been explicitly added to the policy of 'deterrents' and it is not part of Western policy today.

The third means so far used for stopping the further spread of communism is the creation of defensive military organisations. The object of these military organisations is to link together the countries which are in the immediate vicinity of, or not far from the communist world.

The first of these was the North Atlantic Treaty Organisation, created in 1948, and comprising fourteen countries, from Canada to Greece and Turkey. In this way the communist world was ringed round—from the North Pole, from Alaska, down to the Black Sea and the Caucasus—with an uninterrupted chain of countries pledged to go to war against it if any one of them is attacked.

N.A.T.O. has its own forces and conducts manœuvres in which contingents from each of the participating countries take part. In Europe only Sweden and Switzerland have long traditions of neutrality which explains their reluctance to join N.A.T.O. But both these countries are functioning democracies and it is hard to believe that they would surrender their liberties to communist pressure without fighting back. Finland is in a *sui generis* position, with an enforced one-sided neutrality, since her independence depends on Russian goodwill. Finland is virtually a Russian satellite, as there is complete alignment with Russia on all matters of foreign affairs. The Russians are not at the moment pressing their advantage and presumably will not do so until they are ready for the next move westward, because it is clear that there are greater advantages to be derived from an apparent leniency than from outright occupation. The Communist Party of Finland, however, is very powerful and plays an important part in all domestic affairs.

In Asia the democratic powers were not able to create an organisation for defensive purposes as tightly knit as N.A.T.O. There is no military unity of command. There are no pooled armed forces under unified control. The democratic powers, however, were successful in aligning a number of Asiatic countries into the South-East Asia Treaty Organisation. The provisions of this treaty do not include automatic military action by all participating countries in the event of an attack. However, the treaty does provide for consultation with a view to taking defensive common action if an attack occurs, or if subversive activities should lead to a situation where the communists could capture power by force. S.E.A.T.O. is a very imperfect organisation and its military effectiveness remains doubtful. Its membership includes Thailand, the Philippines, Australia, New Zealand, Britain, the United States and Pakistan. The important absentees from this organisation underline the weakness of the anti-communist defence position in South-East Asia. Indonesia, Burma and India, as well as the two small Indo-Chinese countries, Laos and Cambodia, do not belong to S.E.A.T.O., with the result that a possible communist drive in a southerly direction cannot be effectively blocked. In fact, a South-East Asian organisation which does not include India cannot be effective.

The Middle East Treaty Organisation, better known as the Baghdad Pact, is even less effective. The United States, though not a member, explicitly supports it. This area is traditionally a sphere of British influence, since many of the Middle Eastern kingdoms have been created as a result of British endeavour and with active British help. So far, however, only Turkey, Iraq, and Persia have joined Britain in organising this defensive system. Theoretically it provides a continuous, uninterrupted swathe of countries bordering in the West on N.A.T.O., and linked with it through Turkey's participation in both pacts, and in the East with Pakistan and thus, with the S.E.A.T.O. powers. All the other countries of the Middle East have either refused so far to participate in this organisation or are openly opposed to it. Egypt,

Saudi Arabia and Syria are positively hostile to M.E.T.O.
Lebanon tends to keep aloof and be critical of it. Jordan, invited
to join, refused to do so, just after the large-scale rioting which led
to a change of government and, indirectly, to General Glubb's
dismissal. Israel has not been invited. Her application for membership would constitute an embarrassment and would probably
be refused, as no Arab country will today sign a pact with Israel
even if only for purely defensive purposes against a possible
aggressor from outside the Middle East area.

Communism is thus geographically ringed round by systems
which purport to be effective defensive instruments. In reality,
their effectiveness is questionable—to say the least. In Europe and
the North Atlantic the defensive power of the treaty organisation
may be real enough. If put to the test the N.A.T.O. Pact might
lead to concerted action by all the countries concerned.   A
communist attack directed against any of the South-East Asia
countries would probably lead to an immediate international
conference, with solemn denouncing of the aggressor and careful
definition of the measures to be taken if further attacks were to
occur. Aggression there would never be stopped by virtue of the
S.E.A.T.O. Pact, but only if the United States and Britain
provided the weapons and the troops.

To believe in the effectiveness of the Middle East Treaty
Organisation is mere wishful thinking. Turkey is already
organically included in the defensive system of the free world.
The other members of the Baghdad Pact have no armed forces to
speak of, nor any will to stir from their own individual complacency and risk their selfish interests for the sake of rejecting an
aggression which does not affect them directly. A communist
attack in this area can only be stopped by British or American
troops, or both. It is their supreme interest to keep the free flow
of oil from the Middle East unimpaired. Without this oil—until
alternative new sources of supply are found—the economy of

Western Europe, and that of Britain in particular, would be crippled. In addition to these military treaty organisations the Western democracies have signed bilateral defensive alliances with a number of countries. The United States has long had a special relationship with the Philippines whose control they obtained from the Spaniards late in the nineteenth century and whose complete independence they have granted only recently; they are pledged to support it. Similarly, the United States has chosen to endorse the existence of South Korea. And, finally, the United States treaty of friendship with Japan completes the Western peripheral positions along the Pacific coast of Asia.

Akin to these defensive alliances is the special relationship between the United States, on the one hand, and Generalissimo Chiang Kai-shek and General Diem, on the other. Both the military régime of Chiang Kai-shek in Formosa and the off-shore islands, and that of Diem in South Viet Nam, owe their existence to the massive supply of American arms, and, in fact, they would probably collapse both financially and morally without American support. Maintenance of these régimes seems to be of importance for American military strategy.

In a category all of its own is the Western treatment of Yugoslavia. Immediately after Marshal Tito's break with the Cominform in 1948, hopes ran high, particularly in the Foreign Office, and to a lesser extent in the State Department, that Tito's example—if Tito's survival were assured—would be followed by others and thus create a schismatic type of communism, thereby weakening the monolithic structure at the apex of which is the Red Star of the Kremlin. Tito was saved from certain destruction by Western willingness to defend his régime at all costs.

As part of their policy to combat communism the Western democracies have created a number of new agencies, or used several existing ones, for distributing considerable economic help. Through N.A.T.O., S.E.A.T.O. and M.E.T.O. in varying degrees, important sums of money are distributed, not only for military purposes but also to build up the economy of the participating countries, and to raise their standard of living. In addition to these military-economic organisations there are purely economic ones like the Organisation of European Economic Co-operation, the Colombo Plan, or the financing by the West of individual schemes, such as the building of the Aswan Dam, or of steel mills in India.

All these measures by which the Western Powers have attempted to stop the onward, victorious march of communism, have been mitigated by their periodic attempts to come to terms with Russia by direct negotiations. The dispassionate observer of developments since the war must be amazed at the readiness with which the Western Powers respond to the ever-changing mood of the Kremlin leaders. A stiffening of the Russian attitude towards any legitimate Western demand produces a corresponding stiffening in American and British policy, but a 'thaw' in Russia is at once sympathetically viewed. Almost every time the Soviets have shown their willingness to talk the Western Powers have found a way to justify their eagerness to agree to discussions.

Containment, deterrents, defensive organisations, military alliances, direct financial help and economic international organisations for distributing Western financial aid, encouragement of schismatic communism and direct negotiations with the Soviet leaders: these were, and still are, the measures by which the leaders of Western democracy hoped, and still hope, to fight communism. Judged only by the tangible results of their past record they have failed. During the period under review the communists have completed the conquest of China, occupied Tibet, conquered half of Korea and half of Viet Nam, and would no doubt have obtained control of the other half of Viet Nam by the free choice of the Vietnamese people, if the Western Powers had respected their given word, and held free elections in South Viet Nam by July 1956. Judged by the impact which successful communism has had upon millions of people outside the communist world, Western policy since the war must be deemed a dismal and disastrous failure. The professed determination of the West to prevent the spread of communism by force has been overshadowed and largely annulled by countless attempts at appeasement in the forlorn hope that, by concessions, the Western Powers would somehow induce in Russian and Chinese communism a lasting change of heart. It amounts in fact to a hapless policy of linking hands to stem the flood.

This failure of Western policy is attributable directly to two causes: (*a*) lack of understanding of the real nature of communism and (*b*) inability to gauge correctly the appeal of communism to the peoples of the world.

IV

WESTERN ATTITUDES

THERE are three main attitudes towards communism in the West, apart from that firmly held by the millions of refugees from the communist world. First, that of progressives, liberals and left-wing intellectuals; second, that of internationalists, Utopian Marxists, 'democratic' Marxists, to which must be added all strictly materialist socialists and the Trotskyites; and, third, the attitude of conservatives.

The first category, the progressives, tend to be blinded by the good features of communism. They point to the spectacular industrialisation achieved by the Soviet Union; the 'enlightened' ethnical policy of communist governments who claim that they have freed all nationalities from foreign rule; mass education and the determination to wipe out illiteracy; the disappearance of the problem of unemployment; the realisation of complete public ownership of all means of production and the destruction of the exploiting capitalist class; and the tremendous power which the communist world, under Soviet leadership, has managed to build up in less than forty years since the revolution. They overrate the importance of such features as, for example, crèches and rest-houses at holiday resorts, which conceal the reality of communist society.

The arguments of the progressive are reasonable enough. If the new society created by the communists can bring about such signal successes, he says, then it cannot be entirely bad. Therefore, one must come to terms with Russia. After all Russia has a civilising mission in certain areas of the world. She has brought material wellbeing and culture to the motley assortment of obscure nations stretching from Kamchatka deep into central Asia and as far south as the Hindu Kush. Throughout this vast communist empire new industries have sprung up, schools have been built, some languages have, for the first time, acquired an alphabet and a written literature. All this proves to the Western progressive that communism, in spite of its bad features in any case emphatically denied by him, cannot be wholly bad. He refrains from criticising communism in explicit terms, lest he should be accused of narrow-mindedness or of subscribing to the 'bogey' of communism, charges which are anathema to intellectuals whose most cherished attachment has always been to broad-mindedness and the dispassionate appraisal of facts. The progressive intellectual weighs up carefully the good features of communism against its bad features, like the denial of individual liberty, the one-party system, censorship and mind control, and on balance comes down in favour of what he calls an enlightened attitude towards communism. As long as the bad features of communism do not affect him personally, do not deny him the freedom of thought and self-expression which he greatly values, the Western progressive often tolerates and even applauds communism in other lands, even if imposed by force. The lessons of history are easily forgotten. The progressive prefers to forget that totalitarian régimes in the past disturbed the growth of civilisation and perverted the human mind although they frequently displayed many good features also. The Pharaohs built lasting proofs of their glory and power and of the advanced technological development of the early Egyptian civilisation; but the great pyramids were built by the sweat and blood of countless thousands of slaves, many of whom perished in the process.

Alexander the Great pushed the boundaries of his empire to the utter limits of the known world. Attila and Ghenghis Khan conquered the East and threatened the existence of the West. These conquerors achieved tremendous power. If the power, which the Soviets have similarly built up in such a short time, can inspire in us both awe and admiration of their system of government, then we should come out openly on the side of the state, of the social organism which completely owns the individual members who compose it. Power in itself has no moral quality. It is only when power is used that we can decide whether it is good or bad. As long as one single labour camp still exists in the Soviet Union, no matter how strong the communist world grows, the power of the communist state can only make all right-thinking men, who have the development of mankind nearest to their hearts, wish to oppose it with all their strength. If the social organism brought into being by communism in this century is viewed from this standpoint, then no progressive, however left his inclinations, should allow his judgment to be obscured. Mass education no doubt is desirable, but so long as mass education is used to glorify the state, to pervert the mind, rather than stimulate it to think for itself, it must be evil.

Hitler's Germany wiped out unemployment, introduced the most comprehensive social services in the world up to that time. But these social achievements could not alter the evil nature of the structure which was built by mass perversion of the mind on the assumption that only racially pure Aryans were permitted to enjoy the fruits of the régime and that all 'inferior' races qualified for destruction.

Napoleon's power could not have had a better original impulse. It was vested in the energies released by a social revolution. It was the inheritor of the crusading spirit of all those who wanted to share their victory, in the name of liberty, with all other peoples. But neither this, nor Napoleon's lasting great work as codifier, can justify his subsequent path of conquest and war, which wiped out the achievements of those victories which revolutionary France had won for the benefit of Man.

The good internal features of the communist régime, the great power it has achieved in so short a time, and its origin in a generous impulse to serve mankind, cannot change the fact that communism is tyrannical and evil, keeping countless people in subjection.

The second attitude towards the communist world is character-istic of Marxists of all shades of opinion and of doctrinaire social-ists. They persist in the hope that the communist state is about to change. They are whole-hearted believers in the revolution, as it is natural that they should be. Socialism has been achieved, perhaps not by the means which they would themselves approve, but the revolution has inaugurated a new era for mankind. The capitalist exploiters have at long last been completely destroyed. Economic inequality, which makes nonsense of political liberty, has been removed. Now everything is possible. Now true democracy, where both political liberty and economic equality will become a reality, is for the first time attainable. The 'democratic' Marxists of Professor Laski's type, who view the development of modern society from liberal 'capitalist' democracy to revolution and thence to socialism and democracy, condemn the long period of totalitarian dictatorship in the Soviet State. They consider it as transient and, at any rate in their view, the tremendous gains of the revolution, which wiped out exploitation of man by man, is so great that they will put up with the over-long existence of the police state: sooner or later democracy is bound to blossom out of the communist totalitarian state. Since the denunciation of Stalin by his one-time collaborators, who now claim that the 'errors' and crimes of the past are being corrected and removed, this view has gained in credence and plausibility and is advanced with ever-increasing vigour.

For the Utopian Marxists and for the Trotskyites the bugbear has always been Stalin. Lenin's and Trotsky's revolution fulfilled the laws of history which inevitably led to communism. In the early days of the revolution, the great figures of that tremendous upheaval actually tried to bring about the true communist society, better known in the Soviet Union as War Communism. Beset by the capitalist powers who made war on Russia at that time, their good intentions were frustrated. Moreover, the new society was merely finding its way. It would have been too much to expect the towering figures of the revolution to achieve real communism in one jump. Trial and error were inevitable. But their sights were set right, and surely, they will argue, if only Lenin's plans had been carried out by Trotsky the 'Communist State' would have been achieved. Stalin, however, usurped power, and thereby arrested the normal development of the new society. Stalin alone is to be blamed. Even after his death, the tools he created have succeeded so far in preventing the normal development of the State of the Workers. But the Utopian Marxists and the Trotskyites regard the communist world of today as a changing society. They believe that the forces released by the communist revolution will ultimately find their way to the top and produce the change from within which will retain socialism, planned production, and all the other structural features of Soviet society, but will also gradually bring about the removal of the shackles upon the individual, which are such a signal feature of the Soviet Union. It is inevitable, they believe, that the communist world should progress towards granting the individual ever greater liberty of expression and a far more important participation in the affairs of state. At various stages since Stalin's death they have announced, often in the columns of the most respectable 'capitalist' press, that the dawn of a new era has arrived, only to find themselves confuted by subsequent events. Malenkov was supposed to be in league with Beria to liberalise the Soviet state. When Beria was removed in the accepted Soviet fashion, Malenkov was supposed to have given way to the militarists who won the day, but, nevertheless, to have kept his powder dry for a time more propitious to reform. When finally Malenkov was removed from the prominent position which he occupied after Stalin's death, the Stalinists were supposed to have re-entrenched themselves securely in the position of command, with the help of the army. Yet, almost immediately after, we witnessed the spectacle of benign smiles gracefully and liberally distributed throughout the world by the new leaders, Khrushchev and Bulganin.

Such attitudes and interpretations spring from wishful thinking, for the hope of seeing the emergence of the ideal state of one's first political love dies hard. Once this is understood one realises that the attitude of all such Utopian Marxists, Trotskyites and doctrinaire socialists is born from a basically wrong standpoint. For them Western democracy is a dying form of government. Only democracy born of communism has any meaning. They believe that the established laws of social development will bring an end to liberal democracy as it is known in a 'capitalist' society.

In its attempts to understand the communist phenomenon Western democracy has often appealed to this category of informed intellectuals for their interpretation of the Soviet scene. The result has often been a distorted picture of a Soviet Union constantly changing, constantly evolving new, more liberal institutions, the true 'superstructure' of the basic economic structures of communist society. Such views, frequently expressed with great brilliance and 'expert' knowledge, are largely responsible for the confused thinking which today prevents the West from seeing clearly not only the communist objective, but also the path which democracy must follow in order to withstand and repel the communist challenge. It is a tragedy that such thinking has found so great a currency in the Western world, and has so deeply influenced the policy pursued by the West in its attempt to defend itself against communism.

The third attitude towards the communist world is that of

conservatives. The conservatives of the Western democratic countries are unalterably opposed to communist aims and to the communist method of government. But they recognise power. And the communists not only hold political power in the world dominated by Moscow and Peking, they also have tremendous industrial and military power at their command. Hence Moscow and Peking, together with their respective excrescences, must be recognised, and not only formally at the official governmental level, but also in practice by direct dealings in trade, travel and cultural exchanges. Thus, the malign growth, which the communist régime undoubtedly represents to the conservative democrat, must be accepted, he must enter into relations with communism because in this way it will gradually mellow. For the conservative time is of the essence. As long as his own country is not directly threatened with imminent danger, the conservative will automatically relapse into an attitude of 'wait and see'. Besides, conservative thought in Western democracies tends, not unnaturally, to consider that the greatest danger is already past. Stalin built up communist power and Stalin is dead. His successors seem so much more reasonable. The most genuine conservative democrats have an implicit faith in the power of good and the transitoriness of evil. If only the free world continues to hold fast on to its free institutions, supported by the freely-given allegiance of the vast majority of the population, the West will win in the end. The conservative is almost organically prevented from learning the lessons of recent communist history of conquest. Country after country may have fallen prey to a handful of communists against the wishes of the people, but 'that could never happen here'. The danger is dismissed with an almost self-righteous belief in the strength of free institutions, forgetting that those same free institutions crumbled to ·the ground in Czechoslovakia, where they had been cherished by the people with the same ardour as in the West. They collapsed precisely because the free world was not prepared to defend them. The belief that communism will change its nature as well as its hard face, and live peacefully side by side with liberal democracy, is greatly fostered by the crypto-communist and Trotskyite experts, whose views understandably receive so much publicity. The impact of these views upon informed opinion is disastrous. Every slight concession, every semblance of yielding on the part of the communists is hailed as a great victory for the West and a proof that communism is at last embarking upon the road which will end in genuine collaboration with the West.

This attitude is unjustified. Long ago, in the early days of the United Nations and before victory for communism had been won in China, Vishinsky summed up the situation with his customary mocking brilliance: 'Marxism has achieved victory in one-sixth of the world. Now, some powers want us to give it up. They argue that only this can be a safeguard to peace. This is a monstrous and glib argument. Everyone knows that we will not abandon our policy. It is a fair policy which is a policy of peace. Peace is our main objective; those who want peace should stick to us.' At the 20th Communist Party Congress in Moscow in 1956, the first since Stalin's death, all the main speakers proudly referred to the great victories communism had achieved in recent years. Stalin was denounced and his debunking was completed soon after. The new leaders must establish their claim to power in their own right. They are doing it by repudiating everything Stalin brought into being which is not essential to the communist technique for capturing power and to the communist method of government by force. Above all they repudiated Stalin as a tyrannical despot and now claim that they are the true upholders of Marxism-Leninism. This is the real clue to the so-called 'spectacular' changes since Stalin's death. They are not so spectacular. The new holders of power must inevitably seek to entrench themselves firmly in the Kremlin. They are making such changes

as they consider conducive to that end. But they will not change
the methods and objectives of the doctrine which gives them
power and has resulted in such obvious victories since the war.
In his speech at the 20th Communist Party Congress Khrushchev
pointed out with satisfaction that today the Soviet Union is no
longer isolated but surrounded by a number of newly established
people's republics; communism, since its victory in China, decides
the destinies of one-third of the entire population of the earth.

Yet the West continue to hope that the Soviets will change.
Why should they change when they believe that theirs is the only
way? For them, communism is the triumphant march of the
proletariat sweeping away all remnants of reactionary capitalist
society.

Tyrannical power can eventually mellow. The whole history
of mankind bears witness to this. But never in its initial phase.
Communism is still in this phase. It has not only not lost its
initial impetus and vigour, it actually gathers momentum day by
day. Communist revolutionary ardour still beats in many hearts,
particularly outside the communist sphere of influence. The
leaders in the Kremlin know this perfectly well. They are using it
for their own aims. They have power. By trial and error they
have developed an almost infallible technique for enlarging the
area over which they hold sway. Why, indeed, should they
abandon the power which they now possess or abstain from
further enlarging it by those well-tried methods which have
served them so well in the past?

The Austrian peace treaty is often quoted to prove that the
Soviets are now becoming more reasonable, more ready to co-
operate, and led to the Geneva Summit talks in 1955. The fact
that the signing of the Austrian peace treaty, merely represents a
tactical withdrawal from a country where they had no right to be
in the first place, and a mere shift in the general strategy which in
any case resulted in tremendous ideological communist gains in

the far-flung corners of the earth, is conveniently forgotten, because if it were not, it would make nonsense of the entire Western foreign policy *vis-à-vis* the Communist Powers.

This conservative attitude towards communism is based on ignorance. The true democrat has no particular inclination to embark upon the arduous effort to understand what the present world-wide struggle is about. He gets his information at second-hand. Caught up in the complications of domestic political problems, and faced with the confusing picture presented by the experts, who are often ex-communists or Marxists by training and conviction and have no special love for democracy, the conservative will follow the rule of thumb. Instinctively, he will favour the pragmatical approach. Concerned with problems of topical interest he will overlook the over-all picture, a picture which is constantly present and ever guiding the actions under-taken by the rulers of the communist world. But the attitude of the conservative towards communism is of paramount im-portance today because it is the conservatives—the centre party—who now decide the destinies of the Western world.

To these three broad categories a fourth must be added, for it is gaining in importance. Those who think with Starlinger* will say that Russia is essentially European. She has great dominions in Asia, but her tradition, her inspiration, and her vital long-term interests will compel her to range herself with the white race in the not too distant future. Communist China will soon challenge Moscow's present undoubted supremacy. This Russia will not tolerate, and her answer to the Chinese challenge will be found in a genuine collaboration with the West. This argument is no more than hoisting up anew the danger signals of the 'Yellow Peril' so fashionable in the Germany of the twenties. Informed students of communist affairs have read in Chu En Lai's speech before the Chinese Communist Party Congress in 1955, and particularly in his reference to the need to build up a new China without the generous help of the Soviets, a sign that Mao Tse Tung wishes to steer an independent course. In the same way the South-East Asian tour of the Bulganin-Khrushchev team, late in 1955, was viewed as a bid for influence in the vast, densely populated area of Asia at the expense of China, whose potential power and influence there is feared by Russia. It was argued, and it is still hoped by the people who see a conflict developing between China and Russia, that the prospect of a powerful, expanding, industrialised China—pressing hard against the most vulnerable part of Russia's Asiatic frontier where the sparsely populated Siberian plains could offer little effective resistance—seriously perturbs the Soviet leaders. There may be some truth in this argument. But hard facts seem to contradict it. The entire Chinese economy is in the process of forced industrialisation carried out with the practical help of Russian machines and Russian technicians of whom a great number are stationed in China. As Robert Guillain tells us, the Russians are to be found in every field of activity, in every sector of Chinese economic and political life. The Soviet pattern in consolidating power, by industrialisation by means of *piatiletkas*, introducing land reform and socialisation of agriculture, and so forth, is strictly adhered to. There is a complete identification of Soviet and Chinese foreign policy. And, above all, there is the same communist doctrine as developed by Marx, Lenin and Stalin. The cry of racialism, of the white race being imperilled by the rampant yellow hordes, finds no response in the communist. China is rapidly becoming a completely integrated, centralised communist state on the Soviet model. She depends for her industrial growth, as well as for her military power, entirely on the Soviets. China and Russia march side by side at the head of the triumphant proletariat. Why should they part company? Why should Russia abandon China and side with Europe? For at least another generation China will not be in a position to challenge the Soviet power in any way, and whether she ever will is debatable. It will largely depend on the current leadership of both China and Russia and on their personal relations. On the other hand, it is undeniable that the occupants of the Kremlin, now, or in the future, will continue to try to keep a close grip on the entire communist world. This is in the very nature of communist power and the communist conception of liberating mankind from capitalist exploiters, from imperialism and from colonialism. The leaders of all other communist countries are now and will always be required to line up with Moscow. Where is the evidence that Mao Tse Tung or Chu En Lai are steering a different course from that of Moscow? Chu En Lai's demands that the Chinese increase their efforts, and cease to depend on generous Soviet help, which is gratefully and generally acknowledged, is perfectly in keeping with the propaganda line pursued in every other satellite country. More effort is wanted of all workers in the vast 'liberated' world and each region must develop its own local resources and not be a burden on any other. Bulganin's remark to the Indians, when he saw that an American was in charge of a great dam project, is singularly revealing: 'You must do it yourselves. We shall help you to do it yourselves.'

Footnote from p. 38.

  *Well-known German author of *The Limits of Soviet Power,* said to have greatly impressed the German Chancellor, Dr. Adenauer.

V

'HISTORY DECREES'

AN almost equally important contributory factor to the failure
of Western policy *vis-à-vis* communism is the profound
inability to gauge correctly communism's appeal today:
first, within the Western world which is, broadly speaking, inspired by liberal democracy; and, secondly, in the many countries overseas, outside the present sphere of communist influence,
where democracy has never been practised and seldom understood.

The assumption which rests at the very foundation of Western
policy since the war is that poverty breeds communism. Remove
poverty and the danger of communist penetration will be removed with it. This is basically correct. Poverty is the greatest
single weapon in the communist armoury. But it is far from
providing the whole answer. If it were so how can one explain
the steadily growing hard core of active communists both in
France and Italy; the persistently high number of votes which the
Communist Party received in consecutive elections in both these
countries, in spite of a greatly improved economic situation over
the years, with rising standards of living affecting all strata of
society? The communist leader is never the downtrodden pauper
with nothing to lose but his chains. The facts speak for themselves. The Western democracies must be made fully alive to the
danger that their very existence is threatened as long as, and
wherever a communist party exists, no matter how small. Which
country can claim not to have one? The history of communist
conquest in Eastern Europe has taught us that if conditions are

favourable, the illegal, banned handful of communists can spring to instant action and assume the powers of government without any hesitation.

In Western Europe itself the immediate danger is not so great. So long as the danger is realised and Western policy towards communism as a whole is such that no new communist attempt to capture power could go unchallenged, the democratic forces of Western Europe, rent and weakened through internecine strife though they may be, can still be relied upon to defend democracy's existence, even in countries with such powerful communist parties as France and Italy.

Communism's appeal to the rest of the world, in countries where democracy as it is understood in the West has never been practised, presents an entirely different problem. There are no indigenous democratic forces strong and coherent enough to defend the liberties which have never yet been won. To the 'uncommitted' people of the world, as distinct from their governments, communism is a way of life as foreign and as unreal as democracy. They will listen with the same indifference, growing interest, or utter unconcern to the advocates of democracy in their midst as they will listen to those preaching communism. They will be recruited for, or perhaps only swayed by one or the other of the two contending philosophies according to its ability to provide an immediate material benefit. The main problem of the entire 'uncommitted' world is the problem of poverty. Here, unlike Europe, poverty as a factor comes into its own. Around poverty the battle will be fought. The communists promise to cure it quickly by rapid industrialisation. They maintain it is the *only* cure. The indigenous democrats have nothing to offer in exchange but pious statements about liberty and the dignity of man, which to the pariah of an over-populated country must sound hopelessly hollow. So far, the Western countries, with the highly successful but very limited exception of the Colombo plan, have taken only haphazard, even though costly, action.

Before any advance towards a successful Western policy can be made it must be realised that communism holds no terror for the uncommitted people of the world. They are not afraid of it; neither of its totalitarianism and the police state which it invariably establishes, nor of the mind control which it practises, so abhorrent to the educated. The vast majority of these people are still illiterate. They can barely scrape a living today. When communist ideas reach them, which is certain to happen in the next few years as a direct result of Moscow's and Peking's deliberate policy, there is a grave peril that they will turn to communism unless they can be convinced that better results can be achieved in a different way.

Communism is ideally suited in our age for establishing a new form of imperialism, of world conquest. By its doctrine and practice it can claim unblushingly that it is the only way of life capable of establishing a lasting peace, once all capitalist states have been destroyed. It brazenly claims that it is the only form of government giving unhesitating recognition to the full rights of every ethnical group. Communism is the true faith; the unalterable and inescapable *laws* of social development. The communist state is the next unavoidable stage of society. Hence diversity in uniformity. Every nation, every state must sooner or later turn communist. Once communist power is established and uniformity achieved, diversity is encouraged. All ethnical groups are recognised, their languages and institutions studied, preserved and encouraged, as long as they do not run counter to the general trend of political development according to the Marxist-Leninist laws. Viewed in this way, communism presents a direct and strong appeal to all under-privileged ethnical groups whether they be semi-recognised, as in Algeria, or in the newly independent India, or, like the Kurds, squashed between several despotic countries, their claims to national existence unheeded. In his *Memoirs*, Sir Winston Churchill deplores the break-up of the Hapsburg Empire, which he considered an important force for peace and stability in Europe. No doubt it was. But the Austro-Hungarian Empire meant tyrannical rule for the subject peoples who far exceeded in numbers their Austrian and Hungarian overlords. It was these subject peoples who broke up the empire at the first opportunity. The same applies today in the world at large. The subject peoples of the earth will turn to communism unless they can see a better way out for themselves.

Communism fosters the idea of self-respect. It is entirely free from the taint of racialism. Is it surprising, then, that the Cape Coloured turn to communism in great numbers? Let there be no delusions. The intelligent non-white watches intently the progress of racial discrimination in the United States and in the various European empires. Can he hope to achieve one day equality with the white race on the basis of present Western policy? Should he not now turn to communism? Through communism, he is told, he can have racial equality tomorrow, for the asking.

Whenever Moscow makes a statement of policy involving different nationalities and states, the idea of non-interference is proclaimed. To the people to whom it is addressed, outside the present confines of Soviet power, it is absolutely immaterial that this non-interference only operates on condition that complete obedience to Moscow is observed. This they are not told. But it makes no difference. The constant reiteration of the principle of non-interference leaves its mark.

The need for self-respect, so profound in every human heart, is also catered for in communist ideology by the concept of the classless society. Through communism every human being is socially equal to every other. Social equality has not yet become the battle-cry of communism except by implication, but com-

44

munist propaganda already makes indirect use of this idea. Democracy, it says, can never hope to achieve it. Its appeal to rigidly stratified societies like that of India or some of the feudal Arab countries, cannot be denied, although its impact is not yet very apparent.

But the most powerful appeal to all uncommitted nations remains the well-tried slogan: 'Away with colonialism—death to the imperialist exploiters.' Bulganin's speech in Burma in 1955 shocked the West, but it made every Asian and African heart rejoice. He skilfully reasserted Burma's right to self-respect, even greatness, and chastised the new-comers on to the world stage—meaning the British—and condemned them as ruthless exploiters. This is a relatively civilised attack compared with the intensive propaganda that is having such an effect in Asia, Africa and in Latin America as well, where Yankee supremacy is deeply resented.

It is high time the Western world woke up to the fact that Soviet policy today is directly geared to the conquest of Asia and Africa, while holding the West at bay by means of an uneasy truce. An article in *Rude Pravo*, the organ of the Czechoslovak Communist Party (26th January, 1956) proclaims with unusual candour the crumbling of Western power and influence in the whole of Asia and Africa. The historical process of the rebirth of new nations throughout this huge area is noted with approval. 'The national liberation movement of the colonial and dependent countries was born, in the course of centuries, from the smallest sparks of resistance. Under the influence of the great October socialist revolution it grew into the flame of a mighty revolutionary fire, which now shakes the world system of colonial imperialism. . . . The spirit of the Bandung Conference, which developed into a tribunal judging colonialism, is influencing the policy of India, Egypt and other states, remarkably changing the international atmosphere. These changes testify to the deep disintegration of the colonial system.'

VI

PURSUIT OF POWER

COMMUNIST Russia has developed techniques for capturing power and of government by force. Both have been tested in action in country after country and have proved adequate. They are now part and parcel of the *dogma recepta* of communism. Immediately 'objective' as well as 'subjective' conditions favourable to revolution are present a bid for power is made. There are four phases. During the first, the Communist Party enters into a government coalition with other elements, other parties, only to destroy them. The second phase begins when the leaders of the other parties have been removed as traitors, enemies of the people, tools of imperialism. A mock coalition is formed with new men, in league with the communists, masquerading as the leaders of the old parties. A general attack is launched on all institutions which have arisen from an independent national life. Agrarian reform is introduced and the land distributed to the peasants. In the third phase, the other political parties are jettisoned and the Communist Party openly assumes full power. Nationalisation of all means of production is carried out. Religion is attacked and the organised churches are either destroyed or made to serve the godless, materialist state. The bourgeoisie is ground down, eliminated or re-educated in slave-labour camps. The police state is firmly established. The Party assumes complete control of the entire national life. All contacts with the 'capitalist' world are severed. The fourth phase begins formally by the proclamation of a 'people's republic', a state of workers and peasants. A party purge is carried out and all 'national' communists are eliminated. Collectivisation, so far only voluntary, is stepped up and the peasants are deprived of their recently acquired land. The development of the entire economy of the country is planned so as to fit into the over-all communist strategy as directed by Moscow. Moscow's *fiat* becomes law. A final phase, that of formally joining the Union of Soviet Socialist Republics, may or may not follow, according to circumstances and expediency.

The effectiveness of this technique for capturing power is terrifying. Without outside help those who were in command before the communist *coup* are now powerless. The various social forces present in every organised state are adroitly played against each other, and the communists, now in alliance with one, now with another, quickly destroy them all.

The communist method of government by force is also successful. The all-powerful state, firmly in the hands of trustworthy communist cadres, permeates every sector of national life. The secret police, as opposed to the open, uniformed 'militia', entrusted with the maintenance of public order are the eyes and the ears of the régime. Their business is to ensure that no opposition to the communist rule, however slight, shall go unpunished. The cry of reactionary, enemy of the people, tool of capitalism and of Anglo-American imperialism, espionage, treachery and bourgeois thinking is again and again raised against all those with a 'putrid social origin'. The silent and the meek are allowed to live their lives in relative peace but under the constant danger that denunciation may bring them a visit from the secret police in the dead of night. More production is the order of the day, every day. Those who work for the communist state are rewarded. Work is glorified. Stakhanovists, 'heroes of labour', those who achieved eminence in the arts and sport, but only in so far as they serve the communist state, join the ranks of the privileged. Soon, not only party members but a whole new body of men have a vested interest in preserving the communist state. Self-criticism, the public trial and the purge become honoured institutions which ensure the complete outward orthodoxy of the entire populace. Trade-unionism becomes the tool of the Communist Party and the state. Modern means and agencies at the disposal of the communist state are so powerful that any attempt at opposition is instantly squashed. Successful internal revolution, without outside help, is unthinkable. The whole state becomes a vast labour camp, supposed to serve the best interests of the people and gradually to raise their standard of living. In practice it only serves the glorification of the communist leaders who single-mindedly apply themselves to the destruction of all capitalist, reactionary forces throughout the world. For this is what the final aim of communism is.

The communist challenge to the world is *complete*, because it aims at the utter destruction of all organised societies and their replacement with the new communist pattern of life as worked out in the Soviet Union. It is *universal*, because it aims at nothing less than the whole world. It is *permanent*, because every 'capitalist' country is directly and continuously challenged.

Communist policy, as can readily be seen, no longer falls into the established, traditional division between domestic and foreign policy. The world is no longer divided vertically into states, but horizontally into two strata: the exploiters and the exploited. The home of the exploited, the proletariat of the whole world, is the communist bloc, because there exploiters no longer exist. They have been eliminated and government has been assumed by the workers themselves. In the non-communist countries the exploiters are still in power. They also must be eliminated. The process by which this is done can best be likened to a well-planned operation for the drying of a fen-land. First, some dams are built and a firm base established. Then skilled workers are sent out to build new dams so as to prepare for further reclamation. As the operation progresses new land is added to the base. As the waters are driven back they become more and more dangerous, so the base must be continuously strengthened and as soon as possible cultivated. Finally, the collected waters are pumped out and the operation completed. During its execution, however, no further advance must be made on any account if by so doing the base itself is endangered, for in that case the whole operation must be started afresh.

The implementation of communist world policy follows four rules in strict order of priority. (1) The establishment of the 'socialist' camp. (2) The consolidation of power there and the building up of military and industrial strength. (3) The preparation for further advance. (4) The 'liberation' of new lands. An advance will only be made when a country is manœuvred into isolation with no prospect of effective outside help. If effective help is forthcoming the project is abandoned and nothing is lost. The preparation for further advance will continue all the time but more important still is the consolidation of power in the already 'liberated' areas. On no account should the base be endangered. If a direct threat to the 'socialist' camp is made all communist forces everywhere are required to spring to its defence. In this way, flexibility, absolute loyalty to the centre, even when isolated pockets of communists are seemingly sacrificed, is obtained; because only the centre can gauge their immediate usefulness for the over-all objective. Unity of command, and a permanent retention of the initiative, are achieved.

The communist world is at war with the capitalists. As long as the capitalists retain power in any country it is at war with that country. It need not be a shooting war. It is a war of attrition conducted by other means. Victory for the communist forces is assured by a gradual process of disintegration. War becomes necessary only when the existence of the very base is endangered. So long as the non-communist world is disunited, confused, without set objectives, it will be ineffective and new ground will be constantly gained by the communists.

The non-communist world can do nothing to change this communist policy. No amount of appeasement can turn the clock back. If it is in the immediate, or more distant interest of the communist cause to appear at any particular moment ready to make concessions and to compromise, the Moscow and Peking leaders will do so with good grace. But no such move is ever considered out of context. Summit conviviality at Geneva is used with a vengeance to shatter Western complacency in South-East Asia and the Middle East. Withdrawal from Porkkala is used for a sustained campaign, aiming at the abolition of all foreign bases, which, incidentally, finds great response in many of the lands where these bases exist. The Austrian treaty is invariably put forward as a token of Soviet good faith. All signs tend to show that the leaders of the West have completely fallen for this propaganda line, and continue to believe in the possibility of extracting important new concessions from the Soviets; the signing of the Austrian treaty proves, so they think, that concessions may, unpredictably, come at any moment.

VII

THE STAKES ARE HIGH

COUNTLESS warnings have remained unheeded. The tragic facts, the conquest of country after country, have been explained away. And rampant communism continues on its dizzy course piling up success upon success. Appeasement is in the very air we breathe. Appeasement is undoubtedly the result of the genuine belief of the Western leaders in the principles which they practise as well as preach. For them *peace* is normal. By concentrating on one dangerous trouble-spot after another they strive to remove the likelihood of war. They make concessions on each occasion and a peace of sorts is established. But by so doing they invariably lose ground. No sooner is one potential *casus belli* eliminated, that another takes its place. The whole process of pacification, at various levels, is restarted. A new settlement is arrived at, and again some ground is lost. And so it goes on. Each time a new compromise is reached some principle cherished by the democratic West is partially sacrificed, tarnished, or abandoned, even if it only applies to a distant, partly civilised country. The loss of face for the West in the eyes of the uncommitted world is often immeasurably greater than the actual position so carelessly abandoned.

No one in the uncommitted world is capable of understanding clearly what Western policy means today. Is the West defending democracy? In that case why have the countless democrats who gave their lives for the defence of democracy been abandoned to their sorry fate, often without a single authoritative Western protest? Why has the West stood by while fully fledged democracies in the true Western sense were mown down? Is the West defending liberty? In that case what is the Western attitude to the aspirations to a free life of the subject people, now living within the confines controlled by the West? Is the West defending the equal rights of nations, and freedom from interference in other peoples' internal affairs? If so, why does the West retain the right to ride roughshod over the wishes of uncommitted nations and justify this by arguments of security in the interests of maintaining world peace? Is the West defending peace? If so, why does the West prepare for war, establish foreign military bases, and maintain troops on foreign territories?

All these Western moves can be explained and justified. Yet, viewed from Delhi, Bandung, Rijadh, or even Santiago, they are contradictory, inconsistent, or outright perfidious. The uncommitted observers will draw their own conclusions. They will believe that the West is waging a selfish rearguard action to preserve the privileges acquired since the industrial revolution.

It will be said that the opinion of half-civilised, backward, resentful people, in the unimportant countries of the earth, is of no particular moment, and can in no way alter the relation of forces in the present conflict. The truth is that there are two vital factors which will weight the scale one way or the other: (1) the decision of the uncommitted world to orientate itself either towards communism or democracy; (2) the decision of those who participate in the political life of the West, but reject it and seek their salvation in communism. These factors are second in importance only to the ability of the West to defend itself effectively if attacked. They are the people who in the next generation will tilt the scales one way or the other. They must be won for democracy, as practised in the West, because this form of government affords each individual the greatest freedom of action the world has yet seen. They must be won for democracy because through democracy each nation is given the opportunity to develop its natural talent according to its own immemorial traditions and can yet respect the right of others to do likewise. They must be won for democracy because only a democracy will never provoke war since the very concept of government by the people for the people makes not only an aggressive but even a preventive war impossible. They must be won for democracy because only in a democratic state is freedom of thought, speech and self-expression in any form, firmly and fundamentally assured. They must be won for democracy because in a democracy Man *qua* Man is the beginning and end of the state. Man is the instrument which creates the state and the object for whose benefit the state exists. They must be won for democracy because only in a democracy are the life and wellbeing of each individual infinitely precious, and the only restrictions imposed are those designed to prevent the infringement of the same rights for his fellow men.

Nor is this all. They must be won for democracy because democracy is the only truly revolutionary idea yet conceived by men since the world began; though democracy is as yet imperfect and constantly changing, it is capable of reaching untold heights of human endeavour in the service of ordinary people everywhere. They must be won for democracy because they are needed to swell the ranks of those who patiently labour to improve existing democratic institutions; because together we can find better and better solutions to the countless problems which beset us—problems of economic greed, ethnical rights, racial relations, and so forth. They must be won for democracy because democracy will give every one of them a better and fuller enjoyment of life, free from upheavals and catastrophes which are in the very nature of all totalitarian régimes, no matter under what attractive names they parade their doubtful wares. But to win them over to democracy the democratic West should be able to

53

draw upon its best spiritual resources and present an imaginative, constructive policy that will have a powerful appeal to the best sons of all nations. Only thus will democracy attract the wavering multitudes now increasingly tempted by communism.

VIII

WESTERN RESPONSIBILITY

THE West must defend democracy at all costs. If attacked we must be ready to lay down our own lives so that our children and our children's children may enjoy the freedoms which were wrested from authority, by hard-won battles through the centuries. But democracy can only be defended effectively if the Western Powers are capable of turning it into an ideal that claims men's freely given allegiance throughout the uncommitted world.

The spread of communism must be halted by preventing the uncommitted nations from siding with communism. This will only happen if the defence of democracy no longer appears in the eyes of many throughout the world as a selfish fight to preserve the advantages which the democratic countries have over the rest. By comparison the West has untold riches at its disposal. Democracy has served the West well. It is only natural therefore that the West should defend it. But if the defence of democracy appears in this light it will make no appeal to the rest of the world. They will say that democracy is good for America and for Britain, and for the other Western countries; but what does it offer the uncommitted world? Only by a bold, imaginative, far-reaching world-wide practical policy will the uncommitted nations decide of their own free will that democracy is worth fighting for; in spite of the pressing claims and overtures which communism makes today to win them to its cause.

The West can and should reject communism because communism is evil. It stunts the human being; it denies those gains which Western democracy and Western society has already made for Man. It is not the power of the communist states that must be counteracted but the power that communism has over peoples' minds. The true nature of communism must be revealed and broadcast throughout the world. As our knowledge of communism increases it will no longer be feared because only the unknown is frightening; and the evil principles which are its very foundation will be made clear to all. But with knowledge of the true nature of communism must go the positive assertion of all the great values and advantages which democracy holds in store for every nation in the world.

The stage is set, the world is the scene. The teaming, hungry millions are the actors. The leading parts are played by the spirits of good and evil. But the spirit of evil, with untold cunning at his disposal, appears in the magnificent garb of the angel of hope. He can use deceit and distortion and all the weapons, apparently good or bad, that may serve his aim, for everything is permitted to him. The spirits of good can only hope to win by a straight, direct, clean fight. No other weapons are allowed him. He cannot hide anything, he cannot cheat, for the moment he stoops to means which are not intrinsically good he has lost the fight before it is concluded.

This is a time for greatness, and greatness is no accident. History has readily offered the laurels of victory to those who have risen to the call of the hour and has cast into oblivion those who have shirked their responsibilities.

The Romans were great, and their empire lasting, because they brought law and order and peace in a period of almost constant warfare. The French were great when they championed the ideas of liberty and equality for all people. Britain rose to greatness because she championed the cause of the oppressed and was ready to serve and fight for the rights of others as well as her own. Greatness cannot be achieved by the pursuit of selfish interests, however effectively this is done. Only by serving others, and defending the rights of others, is greatness well earned and leadership willingly recognised and accepted.

The Western Powers, and the United States in particular, are today called by history to serve humanity. It is their bounden duty to rise to the needs of the hour and fulfil the responsibility which history has thrown upon their shoulders. If greatness is to be theirs they will produce the leaders who will serve the cause of liberty, not only in their own countries, but throughout the world. Then, and only then, will they have earned the respect, love and admiration of people everywhere.

By a well-directed world-wide campaign the communists have tilted the scales for the moment in their favour. The defenders of democracy are presented in an utterly selfish light. They are the imperialists, the colonisers, the exploiters of the peoples of the world. They built up their own high standards of living by exploiting other peoples. Their presence in any country is in itself a proof that they are exploiting the cheap local labour and tapping rich natural resources. They are now cornered by the onward march of the toilers, who range themselves under the banner of the October revolution. They are now fighting to keep their advantages, to keep their privileges. Their claims in the name of democracy are bunkum. The rising nations of the world, struggling to find their identity, have to fight at every stage in order to wrest their lawful inheritance from the Western imperialists. This picture, so slickly and so vividly painted by communist propaganda, can only be disproved by performance. It is the duty of the West to disprove it. By so doing it will win the battle for the peoples' minds.

IX

FOREIGN POLICY

WESTERN policy, facing the communist challenge, has been, and continues to be, a failure. The communists have advanced on a wide front. There is every evidence that they will continue to advance unchecked.

It is inevitable that this should be so. Western foreign policy is still conducted by antiquated methods, totally incapable of solving the problems of the modern world. The communists, on the other hand, have forged an entirely new conception of action which is proving highly successful. They deal officially with the governments of the so-called capitalist world but address themselves directly, over the heads of the governments, to the peoples of the world. The governments of the capitalist states are the exploiters, whereas communist policy is directed at liberating the people who are shackled by their capitalist rulers, and at the overthrow of the governments with which they deal at the official level. In confusing, dividing and eventually destroying them, the communists use every possible means at their disposal, based on the principle of Soviet action which is war on the capitalists, war on the exploiters. They are at war with every government outside the communist world. A truce, when wanted, is concluded; but permanent peace with any country can only be achieved when the exploiters are overthrown, and the country brought into the 'socialist' camp.

This conception is logical and consistent. It offers a clear directive to all communist forces throughout the world; they do not have to seek their instructions at every stage from Moscow, as is

commonly assumed. The broad outlines of the policy are absolutely clear to every militant communist, because—*once the communist standpoint is accepted*—communist policy is completely
free from contradictions. The apparently sudden changes and
shifts of direction, the apparent contradictions and unpredictable
moves, are comparable to the deployment and redeployment of
various military units and to changes in the direction of forces
which a general must employ when directing a battle. Moscow
not only claims this unity of command of all communist forces,
but her right to decide is readily conceded by the overwhelming
majority of communists everywhere.

Western policy in face of the communist challenge is full of
contradictions. It is still conducted by the methods devised and
implemented in the sixteenth and seventeenth centuries. It is
completely off the point, for it rests on the assumption that the
world is at peace and that peace must be preserved.

The result is, as it has already been explained, that all efforts are
concentrated on preventing a flare-up, though the conflict is
aided and abetted, if not directly caused, by communism. It is like
applying a soothing ointment to cure bubonic plague; such temporary relief achieves nothing, the infection merely breaks out
elsewhere.

Western foreign policy is still based on the prerogative of the
prince and his government, on the concept of national sovereignty. But national sovereignty today is, at best, a fiction. At
its origin the feudal lord established his dominion and ruled over
his people with paternal benevolence, or despotic harshness,
according to his temper, but he dealt with the neighbouring
feudal lord as an equal, the exact relationship being defined by
the relative power of the protagonists. The nature of these
relations between equals was in no way dependent or determined
by the wishes of their respective subjects, though, from time to
time, it may have been coloured by them. This was the birth of

foreign policy. The feudal lord was truly sovereign in his land and his decisions were law, and sovereign lord dealt with sovereign lord. With the advent of the modern national state the concept of sovereignty was preserved. The prerogatives of sovereignty were transferred to the head of the state. As democracy gathered strength and the ultimate power of decision gradually came to be placed in the hands of those elected by the people, the concept of sovereignty came into difficulties. Constitutional scholars produced an answer. Sovereignty, they said, was vested in the people. It was exercised on their behalf, by the elected government. An answer not altogether unsatisfactory, in internal affairs. In the field of foreign relations, however, the difficulty has never been and never can be resolved. In the eighteenth and early nineteenth centuries it could still be maintained that each nation-state made all its own decisions regarding its conduct towards other nation-states, and implemented them according to the power at its disposal. Today, the idea of sovereignty in international relations is completely fictitious. Now, no state can afford to ignore world opinion; no state can make decisions without consideration of the decisions and policies of the other members of the comity of nations. Today, no state can afford to enforce a unilateral decision even if it is not opposed by a greater power than itself. The foreign policy of every state today is tempered and, to a large extent, determined by the wishes and decisions of like-minded nations. Had the defunct League of Nations, or the present United Nations organisation, become a reality the decisions of each individual state would have been determined by the conclave of the assembled representatives of all the states. Since these experiments in world government do not yet work, except in certain limited fields, the modern state still retains certain of the prerogatives of sovereignty. But, since it cannot ignore world opinion and the wishes of like-minded nations, national sovereignty in foreign policy is illusory. To continue to conduct foreign affairs as if the state were fully sovereign is, therefore, a contradiction in terms. To continue to conduct foreign policy only at government level, when it is the will of the people which is the ultimate repository of all decisions, is clearly not only a blatant contradiction, but an antiquated survival containing the seeds of disaster.

The preservation of the idea of national sovereignty among the democratic states leads to an un-coordinated, even haphazard, and frequently impulsive reaction to communist moves. Bulganin sends a letter to President Eisenhower. President Eisenhower answers it immediately because it is thought by the Americans that this is in the best interests of all although the British Prime Minister and the British Foreign Secretary are on their way to America for consultations. Marshal Bulganin immediately sends a second letter. The French Government issues a statement implying acceptance in principle of the idea of new Summit talks. Whatever the rights and wrongs of these political moves, they are some of the countless examples that can be quoted to support the view that, although the democratic powers are at one in wishing to defend themselves against the communist threat, they have as yet a very imperfect machinery for co-ordinating their policies. Although they recognise in principle the need for concerted action, the only practical form this action takes is frequent, but often merely perfunctory consultations between their respective governments at various levels and, from time to time, consultations between the executive heads of state.

The present conduct of Western foreign policy is utterly unsatisfactory; so much so that the Moscow-directed communist powers, always acting in perfect unison, are capable of creating havoc among the uncommitted nations. They can always pursue a deliberate, even if not always successful, policy of setting one democratic country against the other. The Western Powers, on the other hand, with the means and consultative methods which they now have and employ, can at best pursue a purely defensive policy. Each major Soviet move produces the need for consultations. A counter-move is agreed upon and then, on the whole, loyally carried out by all Western democratic governments. In order to have a dynamic, positive and concrete democratic foreign policy towards the communist bloc far more is needed. Communist policy, as we have seen, is directed at the people outside the socialist camp, whose allegiance they wish to capture and whose best interests they proclaim to serve. At the government level they deal with the so-called capitalist central authorities. But every official communist move is designed to facilitate their direct policy which aims at reaching the people. The communists are completely consistent about their ideology and morality which demand of them that they should weaken and destroy the governments with which they deal.

The Western Powers do not direct their policy at the people. They deal officially with the communist governments, and pay lip-service to the idea that they can thus establish and maintain peace. If they are serving and defending democracy, why do they attempt to achieve permanent peace by dealing with communist governments, and by so doing bolster them up against the people these communist governments hold in subjection? By dealing with a tyrannical power the democratic countries of the West implicitly abandon those democrats who languish in the prisons and the labour camps set up by the tyrannical power. By dealing with communist governments overtly in order to solve the various world problems through common action the Western Powers recognise them as *legal* governments, representing their people. They abandon, therefore, their right to defend the people who suffer under despotism. If the Western democracies defend their own democratic liberties, but abandon them outside their own sphere of influence, how can they ever hope to convince the uncommitted nations of the sincerity of their purpose, of their determination to serve humanity? The interested, but uncommitted, observer, must conclude that all talk of defending democracy is mere camouflage for a selfish policy aimed solely at maintaining the material advantages which the Western Powers today undoubtedly have over the rest of the world. But the situation is even worse. The Western democratic governments pursue an official policy of coming to terms with the communist countries and of assuring a smoothly-working policy of co-existence. At the same time, the West continues to encourage various unofficial agencies to broadcast attacks on communism. In the eyes of the interested but uncommitted observer such a policy can only earn for itself the epithet of hypocrisy. This must be clearly understood. The policy of guile and deceit, so successfully pursued by the communist powers at governmental level, is not available to the democratic powers who must present a consistent picture of just action in a just cause. They can only offer a better alternative to communism if they prove in action that their foreign policy springs from the people, serves the people, and can stand up to careful and close inspection.

The hypocrisy and the absurdity of the exchange of diplomatic notes between Moscow and Washington, early in February 1956, on the question of balloons would be hilarious if it were not tragic. For some years before, the Radio Free Europe organisation, whose European HQ is in Munich, had been conducting a most effective campaign of dropping propaganda leaflets over Eastern Europe, by means of various-sized balloons. Thousands of millions of such leaflets had already been sent by February 1956. In those leaflets the tyrannical communist régimes of Eastern Europe were attacked and the peoples incited to passive, if not open resistance to their communist governments. Radio Free Europe, it must be noted, is not an official arm of the American Government. The Czechoslovak Government protested repeatedly against these missiles claiming that they endangered aerial traffic. They officially stated, at one point, that one plane crashed after colliding with such balloons, and demanded that the American and German Governments and the United Nations should intervene and put a stop to the launching of the balloons. However, this achieved no result. Finally the Soviet Government took action and addressed a strong note to Washington. The American reply completely side-stepped the issue of the propaganda balloons and went into all the minutiae of the weather balloons which America sends around the world to collect meteorological data. Soon after, at a press conference, the American Secretary of State was at great pains to explain that these weather balloons were completely harmless and that the data collected were made available to all the countries who wished to have them. He added that they circled the earth at such great heights that they could not cause any interference with air traffic; that the international law regarding the column of air rising above any particular territorial state was far from being fixed; and that, in the interests of good international relations, the United States was quite willing to refrain from sending any further meteorological balloons over communist territory. Needless to say the American reply was found unsatisfactory, for the main concern of the communist governments was the cessation of the launching of propaganda balloons.

Such absurd situations are inevitable so long as the foreign policy of the West is still conducted on the old assumptions and with the old methods. It must be realised that this policy of duplicity deceives no one; that it is impermissible to those who wish to light the beacon of democracy so that it shines in every corner of the earth. Such duplicity only serves the communist powers and enables them to accuse the West of bad faith.

X

DEMOCRACY'S OWN GROUND

IT is trite to say that the world has shrunk, that any decision and any occurrence in the remotest corner of the globe is instantly flashed across the rest of the world. The operative unit, today, is the whole world. Yet this basic fact has not been taken into account by the Western democracies in the conduct of their foreign policy. If the contending ideologies aim at nothing short of the whole world, why not conduct one's own foreign policy on a world basis?

The technique for capturing power, so carefully evolved by communist Russia, and the methods by which Russia conducts all the various phases of its policy, are designed to weaken and eventually destroy the power of the non-communist world. There is nothing in the democratic armour today that the communists have not examined closely and cannot turn to their own use. The struggle between communism and democracy is being fought on ground carefully chosen and prepared by the communists themselves. Their technique is specially designed to destroy the effectiveness of all the weapons used by democracy. A continued use of these old methods will lose battle after battle until democracy will have to fight for its own survival. Democracy must forge new weapons, new methods, and take up an entirely new stand suited to the present communist challenge and capable not only of stemming the communist flood, but also of rolling it back.

Western democracy derives its strength from the will of the people, from its free institutions. In its fight against communism it should use the real weapons of democracy. It should abandon those methods which contradict the very essence of democratic principles in practice and replace them with new methods consistent with the liberties which they cherish. The Western democratic states must, above all, scrupulously avoid laying themselves open to charges of high-handedness, perfidy and deceit.

If the allegiance of the uncommitted nations is wanted, why not evolve a policy which would make the attainment of that aim possible? The Western democratic Powers practise democracy internally. The government is freely elected by the people. It is the people who ultimately decide who their leaders shall be. Yet the Western Powers attempt to rally the uncommitted nations under the flag of democracy by nineteenth-century methods. It is not the peoples' allegiance that is wanted but the pledged word of their often totalitarian, despotic governments. Instead of attempting to secure the goodwill and trust of the people, the West has pursued for nearly a decade a policy aimed at enticing or dragooning the respective governments into signing military pacts and defensive alliances. Such pacts, all qualified observers firmly assert, arouse no response and no enthusiasm whatever in the hearts of the people concerned. Quite apart from their doubtful value—since they can be denounced after a change of government—they merely represent a formal obligation without substance. This is neither the language nor the method of democracy in action. These pacts belong to the feudal past. They can be rejected by the people instantly if feelings run high, as witness the riots which led to the 'postponement' of Jordan's considering joining the Baghdad Pact. At best such pacts are completely ignored by the people: or, at worst, actively repudiated by them.

The world is a unit and the battle is for the allegiance of the peoples in all the six continents. It is, therefore, important that the peoples, or at least their leaders, should be drawn into the struggle and be allowed to make up their own minds. The

Western Powers should actively pursue a policy of enlightening the people throughout the world on the issues at stake with all the powerful means at their disposal. If it is argued that democracy cannot be practised when the human material is still backward and largely illiterate the answer is that democracy itself is an educative process. Democracy should at any rate respect their intelligence and their freedom of choice, which they will voice, if given the chance, through their own natural leaders.

In a democracy one is given a position of responsibility not only because one seeks it but because one is freely entrusted with it. The leaders are generally chosen not because they claim to be elected, but because they deserve it. No consideration, of birth, religious beliefs, doctrine preached, or colour of skin, entitles anyone to hold a position of responsibility. The only deciding factor is the trust of the people. In order to deserve the trust of the world the Western Powers must serve the world. If the West could give evidence of a deep and sincere concern for the welfare of the whole world there would be no great difficulty in securing that trust. If only the West could show their genuine concern for the fate of under-privileged communities and actively embark upon a policy aimed at advancing their interests, the West would earn their trust. In our bewildered age most people would gratefully welcome a firm leadership. It is for the West to rise to that leadership through service. The world will follow.

Finally, Western good faith will be judged by its performance. Concern for the plight of distant communities will not be enough by itself. In the final analysis the West must show that they are prepared to make sacrifices themselves in order to better the lot of the under-privileged. Tangible results are wanted. A man's worth in a democracy is judged by his achievements and his works. The West must be prepared to be judged by the world by the same standards.

This is democracy's own ground. From these basic principles a new policy towards the communist challenge must be found; a policy at once imaginative and practical, showing concrete results in the far corners of the earth. If this is done the democratic West will have found the way, and the communist menace—laid bare so that all will be able to see it—will lose its fire and cease to be a menace. A new explosive idea, the only truly revolutionary idea, which is democracy, will have stolen a march and captured the imagination of all peoples.

XI

COMMUNIST AIMS

THE immediate aims of the policy of the communist world could be listed in the following order of priority:

  (*a*) *Consolidation of power in the liberated area.*

In the Soviet Union itself there is a massive industrial effort. The new five-year plan shows quite clearly that Stalin's announced objectives for 1965 are to be fulfilled much earlier and the aim now is nothing short of catching up with, and surpassing, the production of the Western democracies.[1] There is again great emphasis on industrial power. However much one is inclined to discount many of the sanguine claims which Russian statisticians invariably make, the fact remains that Russia's industrial power is only second to that of the United States. Moreover, there are two areas of economic effort in which they have made tremendous advances, advances which the Western Powers were quick to

[1] TOTAL PRODUCTION

			U.S.S.R.		Britain	United States
			1960 Plan	% increase over 1955	1955	1955
Coal (million tons)	.	.	.	93	2	221·6	46
Pig Iron (do)	.	.	.	3	9	12·5	69·6
Steel (do)	.	.	.	68·3	1	19·8	103·7
Electric power	.	.	.	320	88	76·5 *	612 *
(1,000 m. kW)							

* Estimated

Manchester Guardian, 16th January 1956.

69

recognise. If the Soviets are far behind in housing and in the production of consumer goods, all signs indicate that they have already drawn level with the West in nuclear development and are ahead of the rest of the world in so far as technical education is concerned. The new plan not only calls for the introduction of automation in industry on a vast scale, the technical skill required to turn it into a reality is also now mustered. It is reported that about one million eight hundred thousand students attend Universities and Colleges, all of which have a very strong industrial-technical bias. The major educational reforms introduced in the new five-year plan provide for the training of no less than four million graduates, a figure which is far beyond that of the Western Powers.

As for their nuclear development, the 1955 summer exhibition at Geneva has completely disproved the sceptics. The Soviet nuclear development is real enough, and it would be foolish not to recognise it. They have the hydrogen bomb and they are making rapid strides in the direction of producing nuclear power for industrial uses.

China is still industrially backward. It is clear, however, that the plans which they now implement with Russia's help are having their effect. There is ample evidence that important industrial help to China comes from practically every satellite country in Eastern Europe. Large shipments of goods and equipment are regularly dispatched there from the Adriatic and Black Sea ports. Nevertheless, as a world industrial power China can be discounted in this generation. The effort there seems to be concentrated on two immediate objectives. First, the firm establishment of the régime, not only on the mainland, but also in Formosa and the off-shore islands. In other words, the Chinese communist régime aims at destroying the Chiang Kai-shek nationalists. It is significant that the latest Chinese line is a direct invitation to the Chinese nationalists to take their honourable place in the mighty effort to construct a new China. It is even more significant that the man chosen for making the overtures is Chou En Lai, who was largely responsible for maintaining the Kuomintang-Communist alliance in the past. Chou En Lai is the man who opposed the execution of Chiang Kai-shek in 1936 when he fell into communist hands. On June 28th 1956, Chou En Lai, in a speech before the People's Congress, boldly invited the Nationalist Government on Formosa to begin talks for the 'peaceful liberation' of the island. He said: 'On behalf of the Government I declare officially that we are willing to discuss with the authorities on Taiwan (Formosa) specific steps and conditions for the peaceful liberation of Taiwan.'

Secondly, China is making rapid advances towards the collectivisation of agriculture and the elimination of illiteracy. The formation of the collective farms has recently been speeded up. There is evidence that the original plan for the collectivisation of farms took note of the great resistance offered by the Russian peasant in Stalin's drive in the late twenties. The original targets were, therefore, relatively modest. By the beginning of 1956, however, Mao Tse Tung's original targets have been far exceeded. Consequently, the present plan provides for total collectivisation by 1960.

To wipe out illiteracy a new and far simpler alphabet based on Latin characters is to be introduced. Thus the gates of learning will be wide open for all.

The communists of Eastern Europe have been geared to the over-all communist strategy. At the 1956 Prague meeting of the Warsaw Pact nations Eastern Germany was also brought into the general scheme.

'The further consolidation of the entire socialist camp' was the avowed objective of the eight-day conference held in East Berlin in May 1956. All communist countries were represented, China and Yugoslavia not excluded. A 1956–1960 Economic Co-ordination

Plan was evolved, clearly aiming at creating a common communist market. The suggestions put forward by Baibakov, the chairman of the long-term Soviet economic planning commission, were formally adopted. They stress the importance of division of labour throughout the communist area and the dovetailing of the basic branches of the national economies of all communist countries. The East Berlin conference marks, in effect, the introduction of five-year planning for the entire 'socialist camp'.

These developments cannot but confirm that the consolidation of communist power in the 'liberated' area is proceeding according to plan.

(b) Prevention of effective unity in the non-communist world.

This is one of communism's main canons of policy. Hence the unremitting Russian condemnation of N.A.T.O., West European Union, S.E.A.T.O. and M.E.T.O. Above all the communists aim at creating a split between the Western democratic powers themselves, and particularly between Britain and America.

(c) Recognition of communist conquests in Asia.

The Soviet Union has always championed China's entry into the United Nations and unequivocally supported the North Korean régime and the Vietminh. Russia will continue to press for a collective security pact in Asia as she does in Europe which, in effect, cannot be achieved except by Western recognition of communist conquests in Asia.

(d) Recognition of communist conquests in Europe.

At the Summit Conference in Geneva, in the summer of 1955, the Soviet leaders demanded the conclusion of a European collective security pact. Such a pact, in their view, amounted to a

coming to terms between Warsaw Pact countries and those of
N.A.T.O. They insisted that the problem of European security
must come before any question related to the unification of
Germany. The Soviet leaders always virulently attack the
occasional United States declarations about their policy of
'peaceful liberation' towards Russia's satellites in Eastern Europe.
Their aim in Europe, therefore, is the abandonment by all
Western democracies of any policy which might dislodge some
or all Eastern European countries from the communist bloc. The
communists seek the final and formal recognition of these communist conquests by the conclusion of a European security pact.
The various moves which the Soviets have made in the past few
years display their conviction that the Western Powers will
finally abandon the East European satellites on condition that
Russia agrees to the neutralisation of the whole of Germany.
This was, in effect, the import of their unexpected move in
Austria.

(e) Penetration into Afghanistan.

The Soviet leaders' visit to Khabul, in December 1955, is one of
the latest and the only heralded Soviet move to penetrate into
Afghanistan. Much of this penetration has been going on,
barely noticed by the West, for several years past. No visitor to
Afghanistan can fail to see the Russian influence in almost every
sphere of activity. Russian bulldozers and graders are constructing a new road from the Kyber Pass to Khabul, the Afghan
capital. Russian goods are everywhere in evidence. Young
Afghans are offered special facilities for study in the Soviet Union.
Contracts for constructing public works are almost invariably
awarded to the Soviets because they always make an acceptable
offer, frequently well below cost. It has been reported in the press
that the contract for the construction of a large grain storage plant,
for example, was obtained by the Russians with an offer which

was one-tenth of that submitted by the nearest American competitor. In April 1956, the Soviet Ambassador to Afghanistan presented, with a great show of generosity, 15 buses, 77 cases of spare parts and 704 cases of hospital equipment to the city of Khabul. This was a token gesture of goodwill to mark the Soviet-Afghan Pact, signed in March 1956, under which the Soviet Union will supply materials and equipment to build two hydro-electric stations, three vehicle repair factories, an irrigation works, airfields at Khabul and Bagram, etc. . . . The total credit offered to Afghanistan amounts to £35 millions.

And so it goes on. To Afghanistan the Russians are firm friends. They have openly supported the establishment of Pakhtoonistan as a Pathan State, largely at the expense of Pakistan. In fact it can safely be concluded that the communist bid for power is only delayed by some uncertainty in the Kremlin as to Western reaction.

(f) *Gaining a foothold in the Middle East.*

The communist drive in the Middle East amounts to a concerted attack on all fronts. The Egyptian arms deal with the Czechs has been much publicised in the Western press, but it is of relatively minor significance when compared with the weight of the Soviet and satellite export drive in that area. A wide range of goods are steadily finding their way, at competitive prices, into the Arab states. The Hungarians are building two power plants in Egypt, and their tender for the construction of the Helwan Bridge was reported to have been the lowest received. The goods offered by the communist countries range from capital equipment, locomotives, diesel engines, paper-making machinery and chemicals, to motor-cars, refrigerators, glass and china, typewriters, etc. They are ready to take in return cotton, rice, cotton-cakes, esparto-grass, citrus fruit, and all the other Middle East raw materials which have some difficulty in finding ready markets in the West.

74

Diplomatic moves to back up this drive are adroit; they obviously spring from a clear plan as to final objectives. The activities of Mr. Solod, the former Russian Ambassador in Cairo, and his highly successful handling of the Egyptian-Czechoslovak arms deal, are already well known. At the height of the Suez crisis, in July 1956, Colonel Nasser admitted that the deal was concluded with the Soviet Government and not with Czechoslovakia—which, once again, proves the Moscow control of the over-all communist strategy. But Russia has also recently established diplomatic relations with the newly created kingdom of Libya and appointed there an important representative of the stature of Mr. Generalov, the former Ambassador to Australia. In October 1955 Russia exchanged diplomatic representatives with the little-known, backward kingdom of Yemen. On his return from Moscow, in June 1956, the Yemeni Foreign Minister, Crown Prince Emir Seif el Islam el Badr, announced that Russia would finance some economic projects in Yemen and that a Soviet office would be opened for this purpose in Yemen. Towards Persia Soviet policy has been one of alternating the stick with the carrot. Persia's alignment with the Baghdad Pact has been officially denounced as 'incompatible with the international obligations of Persia', and not infrequently indirect reference had been made to the 1921 Treaty, which is interpreted by Russia as giving her the right to occupy northern Persia if there is evidence of aggressive anti-Soviet preparations there. Since the Baghdad Pact is always referred to as having aggressive anti-Soviet designs the inference is clear for everyone to see. The Soviet move *vis-à-vis* Persia, in the summer of 1956, was one of conciliation. The Shah, accompanied by Queen Soraya, visited the Soviet Union as a result of final arrangements made in December 1955, in Moscow, by a Persian delegation headed by Mohammed Saed.

Damascus, the capital of Syria, is the most important communist centre in the Arab world. The fellow-travelling Arab

Socialist Resurrection Party is noisy and influential. Six Iron Curtain countries have trade agreements with Syria. Czechoslovak arms, including fifty German tanks, have already reached Syria.

(g) *Disintegration of Western Europe.*

Under this heading comes the whole subversive activity of the well-organised and powerful communist parties of Western Europe. Industrial action is pursued with much more vigour, in the present phase, than political action. But the two go hand in hand. In Britain, the communists aim at gaining a large share in the control of the trades-union movement. The 1956 communist bid for a merger between the Amalgamated Engineering Union and thirty-one other allied unions, provides the classic example. If carried through, it would give the communists control over one million five hundred thousand members, thus dominating the country's most vital industries in arms manufacture, machine tools, and most other British export industries.

In West Germany communist activity is concentrated on the key branches of industry. The Minister of All-German Affairs published the following figures. There are six hundred communist-controlled 'works newspapers' published in various factories in West Germany. The number of communists elected to the various works councils in the vital Rhine-Ruhr industrial area is steadily increasing. They often control the works already. In iron and steel, mining, shipbuilding, railways and the motor-car industry the communist influence is enormous. Their effort is now directed at promoting the drive for German unity rather than disrupting the proper functioning of German industry. Their power is such, however, that should they change their policy the industrial peace now prevailing in West Germany would completely disappear. In France and Italy the communists probably have a greater control over the trade-union movement than in any other country of the non-communist world. The communist-controlled World Federation of Trade Unions issued, at the Budapest meeting in October 1955, a directive to Western workers to strike against increased productivity. It remains to be seen when the strike weapon is to be used.

On the political plane the communist effort seems to be directed at neutralising the socialist parties in Western Europe. Invitations to Moscow were received by practically all Western socialist parties. Many, including the French, have accepted and made the 'pilgrimage'. Moreover, the French Communist leader, Duclos, made an open offer to the French Socialist Party, immediately after the 1956 French elections, to collaborate with the socialists in establishing a government of the Left. It is clear, therefore, that communist political action in Western Europe aims at reviving the 'Popular Front' idea. But the timing and the exact method to be employed remain to be decided according to the conditions prevalent in each individual country. One thing is certain; the underlying factor remains unchanged: communist power in Western Europe is steadily increasing, particularly in the industrial field.

(h) *'Peaceful' conquest of South Viet Nam and further penetration into South-East Asia.*

In January 1956, Ho-Chi-Minh, the Vietminh leader, was reported to have promised on certain conditions to stop pressing for the implementation of the Geneva 1954 settlement. This settlement, reached in a blaze of publicity by Russia, China, the United States, Great Britain and the Mendès-France Government, provided for general elections throughout Viet Nam by July 1956. It is an open secret that had such elections been held the whole of Viet Nam would have gone communist. It was realised, however, by the communist leaders, that the Western Powers could not have contemplated a further advance of communism in

South-East Asia. As early as January 1956, therefore, their efforts were concentrated on removing the American forces from the area. For this was Ho-Chi-Minh's main condition. He was to abstain from pressing for the unification of North and South Viet Nam for five years, or even longer, provided the Americans left Viet Nam altogether. This astute move failed, but it remains symptomatic. The Vietminh continues, whenever possible, to negotiate in secret with the various anti-Diem nationalists and sect-leaders in an effort to ensure Diem's removal the moment the Americans leave the country.

An example of the communist penetration *via* trade in South-East Asia is provided by Burma. Uyyaw Nyein, the Burmese Minister of Industry, was reported to have said to a London correspondent: 'You know that we wish to maintain your British form of parliamentary democracy, but at the same time neither Britain nor the United States provides us with enough foreign exchange. Consequently Burma has stepped up its trade and concluded trade agreements, not only with China and the Soviet Union, but also with practically every single East European communist country.'

The Russian trade delegation discussed in Rangoon, in the summer of 1956, the erection of a steel plant, a tractor factory and the establishment of the technical institute which was promised as a gift by Mr. Khrushchev and Marshal Bulganin. Burma's economic problem is her shortage of foreign exchange. To obtain that she must export. Timber and mineral ores would find a ready market in the United States, but Burma is primarily an agricultural country, rice forming over 90 per cent of her foreign exports. The Western countries, however, cannot take this rice surplus. The Soviets are all too willing to do so. Hence closer and closer economic ties with the communist world.

This example brings to the fore the great temptation before all uncommitted nations to trade with the communist bloc. All of them, without exception, are lagging behind in industrial development. They are primarily agricultural countries, or producers of raw materials, which together account for practically the whole of their export trade.

In the case of Malaya, the main export products are rubber and tin, both of which have ready markets in the Western world.[1] But the chief exports of practically all the other uncommitted nations, such as rice, maize, cotton, esparto-grass, etc., cannot easily find a buyer in the Western world. Russia, on the other hand, is almost ideally suited to deal with them. Through forced industrialisation, which gives preferential treatment to heavy industry at the expense of production for consumption, the structure of the Soviet economy is such that it can absorb almost unlimited quantities of raw materials and agricultural produce. The argument is often advanced that the Soviet economy can hardly spare enough capital goods for export, particularly now when Russia fulfils such an important role in laying the foundation of China's industrialisation. This argument, however, does not bear close scrutiny. The Soviet Union is today in a position to supply capital goods if she chooses to do so, and she seems bent on taking up contracts for constructing, with her own specialists, factories and power stations in the countries with which she trades. Furthermore, agriculture has always been not only the Cinderella of Soviet economy, but also the sector in which the Moscow planners have had least success. The current *piatiletka* provides, nevertheless, an increase of 40 per cent of consumer

---

[1] This statement is only, broadly speaking, accurate. The fluctuations of motor-car production in the Western world—like the curtailing of production in 1956, for example—and the steadily rising competition from the synthetic product, place the rubber-producing countries in an unenviable position. Both the Federation of Malaya and the Singapore Government successfully pressed for lifting the embargo on shipments of rubber to China. The enormous potential market of 600 million people is a constant temptation.

goods. To produce these goods they will need new raw materials. It is very likely that this planned increase will be met precisely by the policy of bulk buying which the Soviet Union is now pursuing and the evidence for which is the trade agreements which she has already concluded with the under-developed, uncommitted nations. It should not be forgotten that the past policy of the communists in the economic field was not always based on the principle of 'trade follows flag', but rather the reverse. Sinkiang and Outer Mongolia, in the twenties and thirties, offer almost the classic examples. When the whole economy of these two countries was firmly redirected towards the Soviet Union, their independence became a sham, and their incorporation into the U.S.S.R. became perfunctory, depending on Moscow's decision taken solely on grounds of political expediency.

The policy pursued towards the rest of South-East Asia is a reflection of the principles established at the Bandung Conference in April 1955. Racial segregation was deplored, colonialism and imperialism were denounced. Respect for the sovereignty and territorial integrity of all nations, as well as the equality of all races and all nations, large and small, are the main planks of this policy. In other words, a determined bid to gain the confidence of all South-East Asian people, most of whom, until recently, were ruled over by the West, and all of whom still have a lingering inferiority complex vis-à-vis the 'white' Western Powers. The South-Eastern Asian leaders are fêted in Moscow, Nehru is given fulsome tribute in the communist press, U Nu, the former Burmese Prime Minister, is treated with a deference out of all proportion to the importance of his country. High-ranking Soviet and Chinese officials pay frequent visits to all South-East Asian countries even when they appear to be firmly aligned to the Western Powers, like Pakistan. Norodom Sihanouk of Cambodia, long presented in the Western press as a wise 'democratic' leader, re-orientates his country's policy; visits Moscow and

Peking ('There are two Chinas, but the only China to which Cambodians go is communist China'); embraces *Panchashila*, the 'Five Principles' of co-existence first enunciated in an agreement between India and Communist China on Tibet in 1954; and accepts Soviet 'technical and economic assistance without any mercenary conditions'. A half-brother of the Prime Minister of Laos is the leader of *Pathet Lao*, the communist army which controls the two northern provinces of that country. Even Thailand, thought to be immune to communism, is incapable of resisting the pressure and attraction exercised from, and by, the communist world. In May 1956, the Soviet Legation in Bangkok and the Siamese Legation in Moscow were raised to embassy status and in June 1956 the Thai Government announced the resumption of 'normal trade relations' with communist China.

In their effort to gain the confidence of the present South-East Asian leaders the Moscow and Peking directors of communist world policy may seem to abandon the immediate interests of the various local communist parties. Those communists, who have yet to learn the ways of Moscow and of modern communism in action, baffled and hurt by Moscow's policy, might wish to secede just as a branch of the Communist Party of India has done. This temporary outward setback to the organised communist parties of South-East Asia should not, however, confuse the leaders of the West. The whole of South-East Asia can boast of genuine, well-trained, fanatical communist parties. In Indonesia, for example, there are no less than six different groups, who unashamedly march behind the hammer and sickle of the Partia Komunis Indonesia.

Asian communism has its origin in the great Universities of the West. Back in their countries of origin these Western-trained communists embarked upon their political careers. Today, however, the apron-strings of the West have been severed. They look for guidance direct to Moscow and Peking.

All these communist nuclei in South-East Asia are well-tempered instruments to be brought into action when wanted.

(*i*) *Creating turbulence and unrest and anti-white feelings throughout Africa.*

There is evidence, some of it officially disclosed by the present governments of Africa, that the consular staffs of the Soviet Union cultivate contacts with subversive elements, particularly among coloured Africans and Indians. Communist propaganda is particularly directed towards the Bantu population. The Government of South Africa, for example, served notice to the Soviet authorities and requested that all Soviet consulates in South Africa should be closed and the staffs withdrawn by March 1956. The enormous importance which the Soviets accord to their diplomatic mission in Addis Ababa has already been mentioned. The statement made by Mr. Volkov, the Chairman of the Council of the Soviet Union, leaves no doubt that Soviet relations with Liberia, and with other territories in Africa, will be greatly intensified.

Under the guise of establishing legitimate diplomatic and economic relations the Soviet Union creates the channels necessary for studying the problems of each country in Africa, however unimportant, and for preparing the ground for a further advance of communism.

(*j*) *Breaking away of Germany from the West.*

Informed observers now recognise that Russia's conclusion of the peace treaty with Austria, and the ending of military occupation there, was primarily designed to set a pattern for the solution of the problem of Germany. This course of action for Germany has since been forcefully pursued at all international conferences. Faced with the intransigence of the Western Powers, who would not agree under any circumstances to the establishment of a neutralised Germany, even if united, but insisted that Germany should be allowed freedom of choice after reunion, the communist policy has shifted its ground. Direct negotiations with the Germans became the order of the day. Adenauer went to Moscow. Zorin, the specialist in subversion who brought about the fall of democracy in Czechoslovakia, was sent to Bonn only to be recalled when cold-shouldered by the aged chancellor. Today, all communist efforts are directed against Germany's becoming an integral part of Western Europe. The neutralist elements are encouraged. Preparations are now being made for a later day, when new leaders will be in power in Germany, leaders who may not be averse to following the path of Rapallo, which spells direct dealing with Moscow.

Molotov has clearly stated that the task facing all Germans is to see that West and East Germany pursue the path of 'negotiations and friendly co-operation'. The returning Soviet leaders from the Geneva talks, markedly stopped in East Berlin and firmly declared their intention to uphold 'the social gains' already achieved in the German People's Republic. Molotov's successor, Shepilov, stepped up this policy. Moscow now insists on direct contact between the two halves of divided Germany. Unity can be bought direct from Moscow presumably on condition that it would accept neutrality. At a later stage, an all-German Government, with important communist participation would see the advantages of drawing ever closer to the Soviet Union. This line of action received added point from the Soviet commander in Berlin who declared early in 1956 that East Berlin is part of Eastern Germany and no longer an occupied territory. He also served notice that Berlin is to be the capital of East Germany. This blue-print for German unity is still rejected by the West German Government. There are plenty of signs, however, that important elements wish to examine it more closely. After the failure of the Foreign Ministers November

1955 Geneva meeting, the German weekly, *Deutsche Zukunft*, aptly described the situation by declaring that it is wrong for the Adenauer Government to regard any attempt to produce a new and individual proposal as some kind of treason. If the Western Powers cannot secure Germany's unity the Germans are entitled to try to secure it themselves by direct negotiations with Moscow.

Since then the 'Adenauer formula' has been assailed with ever-increasing vigour. Dr. Dehler, the chairman of the Free Democrats, and the B.H.E. Refugee party clamour for an 'active' foreign policy, the first step of which would be the establishment of diplomatic relations with the satellite states. They openly advocate a 'neutral' united Germany in which the social changes in Eastern Germany need not be reversed. At their party congress, in July 1956, the Social Democrats hammered out a policy which runs counter to everything Dr. Adenauer stands for. They want controlled disarmament; reunification coupled with the creation of a European security system; abolition of conscription; withdrawal of the Federal Republic from the 'Western military alliance' of N.A.T.O.; normal relations with the satellite states and investigation of East-West all-German talks. Even some Christian Democrats—Dr. Adenauer's own party—like Dr. Friedensburg, openly advocate the establishment of a 'new relationship' with the Soviet Union. Will this trend continue? Shepilov's smiles may yet prove more successful than Molotov's impassivity.

The important thing to remember about the problem of Germany is that Russia holds the key to it. Only Russia can bring about the much desired German unity. To be sure, Moscow will not allow it unless Germany breaks away, in some form or other, from the West.

XII

THE SLOGANS

THE immediate objectives pursued by communism today are achieved by implanting into the minds of the people throughout the world a few very simple ideas.

The Communist world is the world of peace.

Not only have the communists established complete peace in the 'liberated' area, they are the upholders and the fighters for peace everywhere. One world peace congress follows in the wake of another. Millions of signatures are collected everywhere for peace petitions. At all international congresses, in all communiqués signed by communist powers, the *leitmotiv* of peace inevitably appears. Communism spares no effort to make the dove of peace its emblem.

The communists are the champions of all oppressed people.

The Bandung Conference issued a document so clearly worded and so decisive in its condemnation of colonialism and imperialism that no nation or group of people, labouring under the reality or the impression of its being under-privileged, can possibly neglect it. Even for those who genuinely believe that their salvation can come from the workings of Western democracy, the proclamation of Bandung is a weapon. At the end of his South-East Asian tour Khrushchev reported to the Supreme Soviet that Africa is held down by chains which are choking the people but that nation after nation will rise up in the fight against colonialism. 'We support these fighters for independence and wish them success,' he declared.

Communism alone is capable of bringing about an era of plenty.

Marxism-Leninism is the key to success. Quick economic advance, industrialisation, and national strength, can only come by following the path blazed by the Soviet Union.

These three simple ideas are the three prongs which carry the communist world to success. They recruit the fanatical support of many and the acquiescence of those who see no other clear alternative. This message was already forged in the Stalin era, but the new leaders have removed one of Stalin's dogmas which in many ways weakened the strength of the communist challenge. At the 20th Congress of the Communist Party, in February 1956, Krushchev condemned Stalin's thesis of the 'inevitability of war'. Communism no longer advances by force of arms. Capitalism is condemned by history. One by one the capitalist states will inevitably take the socialist path to communism, because the forces now at work in capitalist society have decreed it. It is the only scientifically proved, further step for human society. Even revolution is no longer necessary. The new leaders in the Kremlin condemn capitalism, more in sorrow than in anger, supremely confident of the righteousness of their cause.

In November 1955 another Soviet leader, Kaganovich, clearly stated the Soviet desire to bring about a *détente*, but he added that, if peaceful relations are to be established, reactionary imperialist forces must be compelled to retreat still further.

PART TWO

TOWARDS A POSITIVE WESTERN POLICY

I

WESTERN STRENGTH

THE West can and must accept this tremendous challenge, but no half measures can stem the communist tide. The West must stand four-square on the achievements of Western society, on the great advances for the individual which it has already realised. The West must make it abundantly clear that these advances are available to the most humble nation in the world. The West, while admitting its own great material comfort and superiority over all other organised societies, must convince the whole world, and particularly the uncommitted nations, that it is ready, with an earnest determination, to use its material superiority for the service of all mankind. In other words, the West must think and plan on a world scale.

Today the challenge is so immense and the conflict, one could almost say, so awe-inspiring, affecting as it does the trend of future history perhaps for centuries to come, that the problem must be cast in its simplest terms. What, in effect, are the only reliable forces of democracy? The answer lies in the individual. Democracy, as evolved through a long struggle here in the West, will live or die according to whether it can now muster to its defence all those who genuinely believe in it. Pacts and alliances may be signed; countries under various forms of government may be lined up, some of their own accord, others for immediate material advantages. But democracy itself does not reside in the state. However much some states may be permeated with the democratic spirit, the battle must in the end be fought by the individual. If democracy is to emerge triumphant from this grave conflict, which in the next twenty to fifty years will become decisive, those individuals who believe in freedom, in being masters of their own lives, must be made to realise the untold danger of this hour.

The West must openly condemn government by force. It must condemn officially the subjection of all peoples everywhere. Thus, the defence of freedom would become a rallying cry which would produce a response from all those who want to be free.

If instead of making pious and meaningless declarations, the West finds the moral strength to put into effect these high principles, then the communist technique for capturing power and method of government by force will be seen in true perspective, as only one of those evil forces which democracy is pledged to oppose.

To achieve this the democratic states must re-define the basic principles of their foreign policy and re-design it with the avowed objective of reaching the peoples of the world. It must be a policy of concerted action at all levels, capable of matching communist policy directed against the capitalist world, which is, and has been for many years conducted at all levels.

The political action of the democratic governments, and particularly that of the Anglo-Saxon leaders of the free world, must be completely supported by all their economic and cultural agencies, whether national or international.

The policy of the communist powers is based on the assumption that communism wages war on the exploiters now ruling the capitalist world. There can be a truce with those governments which are in the hands of the exploiters, but there can never be peace until the day on which the last capitalist has been eliminated or re-educated.

To face the communist challenge effectively the West must abandon in the first place its much cherished idea that the world is at peace and accept the communist assumption, that the communist powers are at war with the democratic states. If this basic assumption is accepted, once and for all, the first duty of the Western democracies is to make a shooting war impossible. Secondly, they must turn this war, which is waged upon them unrelentingly by the communist world, into open competition. Thirdly, the West must prove to the people of the world that democracy in practice is superior to communism and to all other forms of government, and that democracy alone can confer tremendous advantages upon all those individuals and nations who believe in it and who are successful in making it a reality in their own countries.

Once this basic assumption is accepted, and these three fundamental principles, which spring from it, earnestly pursued, the norms of conduct by which Western policy must abide come into focus almost automatically.

II

COEXISTENCE

THE first victim of such a new conception is the idea that there is one world earnestly struggling to achieve or maintain peace, an idea which underlies all action now pursued by Western statesmen. This idea is erroneous, and must be jettisoned. The world is not one. From the communist standpoint the world is split in two: the communist world and the rest. From the Western point of view it is split into three, not always clearly defined, categories: a solid, monolithic communist bloc; a loosely defined democratic bloc, centred round the Anglo-Saxon world and Western Europe; and the uncommitted nations, which occupy the largest part of the world.

If permanent peace with the communist powers cannot be achieved, because they are incapable of it by the very nature of their power, it is futile to pursue the ideal of collective security. Collective security on a world-wide basis, if entered upon by all powers, will merely help the communist world, as it would remove all danger to itself when communism makes a fresh advance. If a communist bid for power is made in any country, that bid is decreed an internal affair, the collective security agreement preventing any interference from outside. Thus the communists are given a free hand to establish themselves in power. In the same way, European security, which has been the communist aim at conference after conference, will be seen for what it is—a dream never to be realised as long as communism exists. If they are organically incapable of accepting *permanent* peace as long as 'capitalist' countries exist, any pact aimed at securing peace serves only the communists. It removes any danger to the communist states and it gives a free rein to their policy of subversion, of quietly, but persistently making preparations for a further advance of communism. If this is recognised the democratic West will abandon all attempts to sign a collective or formal security agreement.

If permanent peace with the communist powers cannot be achieved, then the West must finally abandon all efforts at ending the cold war. Any such attempts will be identified for what they are: futile and abortive. The West wages no war, but the West must be fully aware that war is waged upon itself by the communist world. A European security pact, or an agreement to end the cold war, would result merely in the final recognition of all communist conquests, and a Western pledge to end all hostility to communism, and give free rein to the subversive activity of communism in that part of Europe which is still free.

This problem of security and of the cold war is a very good example of the false position into which the West has been manœuvred, precisely because the basic assumption, on which the whole structure of Western foreign policy is built, is incorrect. Security is wanted and collective security agreements are concluded in order to bring about a state of real peace. How is this achieved theoretically? In the first place, the agreement must provide for the removal of as many as possible of the trying problems which are present in the area under review. Then the security agreement establishes a settlement which will be respected by the High Contracting Powers. The object of the security agreement, therefore, is to deter any potential aggressor from disturbing the *status quo*. The security agreement, however, is completely useless if the High Contracting Powers lack the will to make it a reality. If one or more of the countries who appended their signatures to the document which confirms the security agreement, are pledged, by the nature of the philosophy

which they uphold, to work for the destruction of the other contracting powers, the beneficiaries of such security agreements can
only be those who break the agreement and exploit the good faith
of the others.

This is precisely the case today. Communist Russia constantly
presses for the conclusion of a security agreement in Europe.
At the Foreign Ministers' conference in Geneva in the autumn of
1955, Mr. Molotov put the conclusion of a European security
pact as the most important item on the agenda. Only after that
would he discuss the question of German unity. *Pravda* was more
specific: it envisaged a treaty between the 'existing groups in
Europe, N.A.T.O. and the West European Union on the one
hand, and the Warsaw Pact Powers on the other'. The conclusion
of such a pact would have given the communist powers two great
advantages: an immediate formal recognition of the present
status quo in Europe, i.e. the communist conquest of the whole of
Eastern Europe; and the long-term, lasting advantage of the
solemn pledge of the Western Powers never to disturb this
status quo. *The Times* of London actually suggested that a temporary security pact might be worth considering even if German
unity could not at present be achieved. This suggestion created
widespread protest throughout Germany, but no one stopped to
think that the conclusion of a European security pact, whether
before Germany was united, *or after*, would in fact only have
benefited Communist Russia. If unification of Germany is
achieved with Russian agreement, and a security pact concluded
afterwards, the true import of such a move would not be lost on
all those people who today believe that the West will stand by the
high ideals which it proclaims. They could only conclude, either
that the West is trading the freedom of all the countries in Eastern
Europe, now held by the communists through sheer force, in order
to secure the unification of Germany, or that the West is guilty of
the same bad faith which can rightly be attributed to the Russians.

Further evidence of the importance which the communist world attaches to the conclusion of such security pacts is contained in Marshal Bulganin's speech in New Delhi, when he reaffirmed the Russian desire to create a European collective security system. On that occasion he suggested that the Warsaw Treaty, as well as N.A.T.O. and the Paris Agreements, should be dissolved—and it is surprising to see that the General Affairs Committee of the Council of Europe presented a plan for the Geneva Conference in October 1955, putting forward this same idea, advocating a collective European security system under which N.A.T.O. could eventually be superseded by a security pact including Russia and her satellites!

The ambiguous position in which the West places itself by continuing to pursue this aim of concluding collective security agreements with communist powers as co-signatories, destroys the entire moral foundation of Western policy. If the West wants to defend democracy it must do so openly, not only in the countries where there is already a democratic régime, but also in the countries in which democracy has been destroyed, but which still struggle to regain it. A collective security agreement can only have value among like-minded nations, who are determined to respect their pledged word and genuinely want to maintain peace. The lessening of international tension and the ending of the cold war can be achieved without any difficulty, not by further concessions from the West, but by communist determination and good faith to end the war which it wages against the non-communist world.

The same arguments apply to other Western actions, which all spring from this admirable but foolish desire on the part of the Western Powers to do everything possible to establish lasting peace, not realising that it is precisely this desire which Soviet diplomacy so adroitly exploits.

The Summit meeting in 1955 in Geneva is a case in point. It

created the 'Geneva Spirit', which in effect can only mean that the participating powers have convinced each other of their essentially pacific intentions and have given each other assurances that in no circumstances will they embark on war. The creation of such a 'spirit' can only benefit those powers who do not intend to abide by it. The immediate consequences in world politics of the 'Geneva Spirit' are common history. The Soviet attitude towards the Western Powers immediately stiffened after the Summit meeting, and the way in which they exploited it to further their permanent aims disheartened even the staunchest believer in appeasement. It disheartened even those who all too readily attribute profoundly peaceful intentions to the Soviet leaders and always advance the argument that the Soviets will settle down in a state of beatific permanent peace if only Soviet Russia's 'search for security' and 'legitimate demands' are satisfied. But even after they used the 'Geneva Spirit' for launching unwarranted attacks on the Western Powers during their Asian tour, the communist leaders continued to exploit it, and invoked it not only in their worldwide propaganda but also whenever Western reaction stiffened and showed signs of displeasure and irritation, in the face of a Soviet breach of confidence. In order to exploit the 'Geneva Spirit' to the full, the communists glibly proclaimed that it lives on; for example *Pravda* announced in November 1955: 'That the "Geneva Spirit" is still alive is to be seen in the fact that an ever-growing number of people in the West demand agreement in the interest of peace and security.'

The Western attitude must be revised towards three other pet communist lines of diplomatic action; otherwise permanent peace with the communist powers cannot be achieved. The communist countries proffer friendship pacts, non-aggression pacts, and agreements for the renunciation of force. In his second message to President Eisenhower, early in 1956, Marshal Bulganin made an offer for the conclusion of a treaty of co-operation and friendship between Russia and the United States and between Russia and Great Britain. Similar offers have been made to a great many countries at various stages in the history of the Soviet Union. The most significant of them is the twenty year Treaty of Friendship concluded by Stalin with President Beneš of Czechoslovakia in the midst of the Second World War. Less than seven years later the import of that pact of friendship, and of all similar offers of friendship and non-aggression pacts, as well as that of agreements for the renunciation of force, had borne its fruit. The tragic fall of Czechoslovakia should have served as a solemn warning for those who contemplate the conclusion of such pacts with communist countries. It is all too apparent that the lesson of Czechoslovakia's good faith has yet to be learned.

Western policy towards the communist world can only hope to be successful if it is based on facts. The primary fact of the world situation today is, as we have said, that the communist world wages unrelenting and ceaseless war against all 'capitalist' governments. Co-existence is the brain-child of Stalin, who defined it more than twenty years ago. It means an armed truce with the capitalist world, until the conditions favourable to a further advance of communism are prepared. Co-existence does not mean peace. All negotiations by the 'capitalist' governments with the communist powers must be conducted from the standpoint that they are two opposing forces; that there is no common ground whatever between them; and that as long as they are in equipoise they can co-exist. But when that extremely delicate and constantly changing equilibrium is seriously disturbed, in any part of the world, the West must know that the communist forces will advance.

On this basis alone, genuine co-existence is possible; a co-existence that will not in any way impair and damage the interests of the free world. Negotiations and agreements between the Western World and the Communist World would be conducted on a strict, hard-bargaining basis; the fundamental opposition between democracy and communism would either be clearly stated or, at least, never concealed; the limited measure of agreement, if it can be found, unequivocally revealed; and the communiqués issued at the end of such meetings would never include high-sounding principles about establishing peace, friendship, unity and all the much-abused diplomatic terminology which has constantly degraded the moral position of the West in recent years.

III

THE UNITED NATIONS

THE United Nations Organisation is the outward expression of the one-world concept, a world united in peace and working for the maintenance of peace. If this concept is jettisoned the nature of the United Nations must assume a new form.

As it now functions the United Nations is bogged down in a morass of contradictions.

In the first place its very name is a contradiction. The nations represented are not united, since the monolithic bloc of the communist powers is firmly and unalterably opposed to the other members. No action by the United Nations can be contemplated unless the communist powers agree with it, because they have the right of veto. Action in Korea was possible only because the Soviets made the tactical mistake of absenting themselves from the debates, but they have learnt their lesson. The usefulness of the United Nations cannot be denied, but it is operative only in minor matters. In all conflicts of world importance it is completely powerless.

The contradiction in the United Nations organisation in respect of membership is even more blatant. Article 4 of the Charter declares that membership is open only to countries who accept the obligations of the Charter and who therefore guarantee the exercise of human rights to all their respective citizens. Yet this same organisation accepted in 1955 the 'package deal' by which, out of 18 applicants, 16 were admitted without any attention being paid to their credentials. In this 'package deal'

99

there were four communist countries, whose membership had been opposed by the West for years, precisely because they did not fulfil the obligations of the Charter. Stranger still is that, in order to get the 'package deal' through, the West had to abandon Japan's justified claim to membership, and pair her with Outer Mongolia from the communist list of applicants. No dispassionate observer can accept the morality of such a deal, or explain it away. He is more likely to be struck by the fact that the West fails to be consistent. He will notice that the principles proclaimed by the communist powers are as inspiring as those proclaimed by the West. He will be aware that the communists fail to live up to them. But how can he distinguish between the two, particularly if he belongs to the uncommitted nations, and has no special love for democracy? If this sort of dealing is openly accepted by the democratic West it is more than likely that the uncommitted observer will decide that there is not much to choose between the Western democracies and the communist powers, because they are two power groups struggling for world supremacy. He will probably decide that they both use the same methods of power politics. Judged by its performance, the stand of the West in his eyes will inevitably be divested of any moral quality.

U.N.O. is supposed to provide the forum in which momentous decisions for the welfare of the world are made. Yet, in view of the chronic paralysis from which it suffers, as a result of the right to exercise a veto which is conferred upon the Great Powers, the United Nations is completely by-passed in all matters of moment to contemporary history. The Indo-China question was settled in 1954 at a special meeting in Geneva, presumably with the excuse that, since Communist China is not a member of the United Nations, special arrangements must be accepted when trying to find a solution to a problem which directly concerns her. The problem of Germany, to quote another telling example, is of direct concern to the whole world. Nevertheless, the German problem has invariably been discussed at various high level talks *outside the United Nations,* presumably because of the claim that it is for Germany's late enemies to decide her fate; but there is no excuse whatever for discussing outside the United Nations such problems as disarmament or European security. All that is achieved through by-passing the United Nations is to lessen its importance and standing as an international organisation. Yet this is just what has been happening for the past few years and the twin problems of disarmament and security are constantly taken up by the Great Powers at conference after conference outside the United Nations.

The communist attitude towards U.N.O. is quite clear. After some initial vacillation they finally decided that the United Nations Organisation provided them firstly with a good platform for disseminating their views to a world-wide audience; secondly, for furthering their aim to create within the United Nations discord among the non-communist countries, just as they do outside it; and, thirdly, for trying to influence in their favour as many as possible of the non-communist member nations.

At no time have the communists regarded the United Nations as a genuine instrument for peace, as a true forum in which the countries of the world can state their views and do their best to remove any cause of friction. At no time have the communists displayed any desire to use the United Nations either as the supreme arbiter in international conflicts; or as the chosen, exclusive instrument through which the conflicts inevitably arising in the world can be brought nearer to solution within the limits set by realities. Having secured the paralysis of the United Nations, through their insistence on exercising the right of veto on all important occasions, the communists proceeded to make excellent use of it on the lines described above.

Instead of appraising correctly the communist attitude towards the United Nations and then acting upon it, the Western Powers with touching persistence have clung to the idea of turning the United Nations into that effective instrument for peace which it was meant to be in their original design. This conception springs from the Western belief that the world is one, united, in securing and upholding peace. The result was inevitable. From a position of untold strength at the end of the war, when the West could muster almost unanimous support outside the communist bloc countries, the West has sunk today to a doubtful position. Its moral leadership is challenged. Its good intentions are questioned. And, since Bandung, we have seen the emergence of the Afro-Asian bloc which can command such a large number of votes among the uncommitted nations that the West is often placed in the minority. The wisdom of Krishna Menon prevented an open clash in 1955 over the North African question, but the French delegate was forced to stalk out of the General Assembly when Algeria was about to be placed on the agenda, and Britain saw no other way out of her unenviable position but to support France's attitude.

Has the West sufficient courage to face reality in its stark nakedness? If so, Western democratic leaders must realize that the communist powers have used the United Nations for their own purposes with signal success. This they have achieved because their objective is clearly defined, their methods of operation were quickly worked out and then consistently applied.

The Western attitude towards the United Nations can only be described as one of utter confusion; there is evidence of this confusion in the definition of the important function which the United Nations is meant to fulfil. To begin with, the Western Powers have given way to the Soviets and accepted their proposal that the right of veto should be the apanage of the Great Powers. Nevertheless, they have never spared any effort to make the United Nations an effective organisation for peace. But, instead of pursuing a policy completely in keeping with this purpose, the Western Powers themselves struck at the very foundation of the organisation by agreeing to negotiate with the communist members of the United Nations outside it whenever a matter of great importance came up. It can be argued that there was nothing else to be done, since all important decisions were blocked by the Soviet veto. This argument cannot hold water. The Great Powers could have refused to negotiate outside the United Nations and stood unflinchingly by that decision. The Soviets would then have had to negotiate within the United Nations or not negotiate at all. One example will suffice to show the impossible position in which the West has placed itself by this very contradictory policy towards the United Nations.

The West is very anxious that Russia should be kept out of the Middle East. Russia has never yet had an important say in Middle Eastern affairs and, until recently, never claimed it. When the Jewish-Arab conflict turned into a war the Western Powers attempted to bring hostilities to an end. They reached agreement and made the Tripartite Declaration in which they served notice on all concerned that they would intervene against the power, or powers, who sought to change by force the 1949 armistice borders of Israel. Since 1954 the Soviet Government has given material and conclusive proof that it intends to take an active part in Middle Eastern affairs. When the Egyptian-Czechoslovak arms deal was followed by a number of border skirmishes, with violent Israeli reprisals, there was widespread anxiety lest the Arab-Israeli conflict would once again flare up into a full-sized war. To prevent this the Western Powers once again issued official statements confirming their determination to stand by their Tripartite agreement and to intervene against any aggressor. By this time, however, the Soviet position in the Middle East had materially altered. According to Western estimates Soviet-Egyptian trade—mainly cotton, rice and onions in exchange for Migs and tanks—had increased in 1955 by 250 per cent over the corresponding figure for 1954. Only a few weeks before, economic delegations from the Soviet Union toured the Middle Eastern capitals apparently with full authority to enter into trade negotiations with the Arab countries. Offers of arms, it was reported, had been made to Syria and Saudi Arabia and the fact that the Soviets had offered the Libyan Government economic assistance was not denied by the Libyan Prime Minister, Mustapha ben Halim. In February 1956 when the Western Powers reasserted their determination to enforce the 1950 Tripartite Declaration, the Soviet Union departed from its customary reticence on matters of Middle Eastern concern; it at once argued that any Western intervention in Middle Eastern territory was illegal unless specially sanctioned by the Security Council of the United Nations. Mr. Kisselev, the Russian Ambassador to Cairo, declared on February 25th 1956, that the 1950 Western Tripartite Declaration on Israel, which was re-affirmed in February 1956 by the Washington Declaration, was without any value. In other words, the Soviets made it plain to all who understand Soviet communiqués that they would not countenance any intervention in the Middle East, except with Soviet agreement and Soviet participation. They claimed, in fact, the right to have a say in Middle Eastern affairs. The State Department rightly stated that the 1950 Tripartite Declaration provided for the Three Powers 'to take action *both within and outside* the United Nations under certain circumstances'; and argued, with far less justification, that such an action 'outside' the United Nations should be compatible with United Nations obligations. The American spokesman was claiming, in fact, that a declaration, made entirely outside the United Nations and in disregard of its Charter, is sufficient justification to permit armed intervention by the powers concerned. This, of course, is an absolutely untenable position. Either the United Nations is an effective organisation, which alone can determine when and where any member or members of the United Nations should intervene in order to prevent or stop aggression, or the United Nations has no say in these matters at all. If the intervention in the Middle East is legal, according to the 1950 Tripartite Declaration, then it is clearly legal for Russia, China and, say, North Viet Nam to issue a tripartite declaration that they will intervene against any aggressor who disturbed in any way the peace in South-East Asia.

These are the three main contradictions which vitiate the very nature of the United Nations as conceived by the West. First, the United Nations is not a forum for securing and maintaining peace; it is not, in fact, a 'united' nations organisation. Secondly, the United Nations is not an organisation of like-minded countries abiding by the provisions of Article 4 of the Charter; it has member countries who accept those obligations and guarantee the respect of human rights to all their citizens, but it also has member nations who completely ignore or openly violate those provisions. And, finally, the United Nations is not an effective organisation for peace because the will to make it so is signally absent in a great many of its member states, one of whom also exercises the right of veto.

These contradictions have been of service only to the communist powers. They make the Western democracies appear hypocritical and dangerously confused. In order to evolve an effective, consistent Western policy, which would stand close scrutiny of its morality, the conception of a United Nations capable of securing real peace and effectively working for the maintenance of peace must be abandoned. This is not to suggest that the United Nations itself should be abandoned. Neither is it suggested that the United Nations is valueless as an organisation, nor that the present importance and effectiveness of the United Nations such as it is, should in any way be lessened. The value of the United

Nations is recognised as real but limited. And it is argued that the realities of the United Nations, as it now functions, should be fully accepted and openly proclaimed. In this way the West would cease to be a party to the present conspiracy of deception.

Why not let the United Nations function on the lines of a state parliament? There are two obvious and immediate objections. First, the United Nations cannot function as a parliament because its members are nominated and not elected; and, secondly, because to turn the United Nations into a parliament would be to anticipate the creation of a world parliament before the world is fit to have it.

Both these arguments are valid. But there is no need to attempt the creation of a separate world parliament, the expression of the world popular will. The United Nations as it is now constructed could remain materially unaltered. Only the fiction that it is the forum of peace-loving nations would be removed, and the reality of the international situation fully accepted.

This could be done by considering the United Nations, for want of a better name, an *agora* (the Greek word for 'forum') in which each country, without exception, would qualify for membership, irrespective of its type of government or régime. In this way the difficulties and the contradictions pointed out above, damaging only to the reputation of the West, are completely removed. Why not have Outer Mongolia, Japan, or any other country? All applicant countries should be eligible. The West should declare this openly and then proceed to accept any applicant nation, provided it has an executive authority vested in a recognisable government, irrespective of the methods by which the government came to power. If the Soviets were then to block Japan or any other country, it would be exclusively for them to justify their action, with the corresponding loss of prestige if their arguments were unsatisfactory.

The West should abandon the fiction that significant action in world affairs can and should be taken only through the United Nations. If action in the interest of peace can be taken by and through the United Nations, such action should be greatly welcomed and applauded. If not, the West should declare unequivocally its intention of taking action in defence of democracy outside the United Nations and strictly abide by this intention in practice. Again, by adopting such a clear-cut attitude the present contradictions and illogicalities of, for example, the Arab-Israeli conflict, would be removed. All action taken by the Western democracies outside the United Nations would be justified precisely because when peace and democracy are endangered they defend them. No other justification should be sought. The defence of peace and of the liberty of the free institutions of democracy would be sufficient justification for drastic action in the eyes of the world.

The Western Powers should then proceed to transform this *agora* into the theatre where the twentieth century world struggle for the Allegiance of Man is staged. Let democracy face and openly challenge communism in this *agora*, instead of reluctantly accepting the insidious and mercurial communist challenge elsewhere.

By changing thus the basic conception of the United Nations the battle between Communism and Democracy would be fought *with the weapons of democracy* before an interested world audience. The struggle would no longer be conducted by infiltration, treachery and deceit, but by open debate, which should be given the widest possible publicity. Every communist lie should be nailed down as it invariably would be in a parliament where democracy works. There are still very few democracies that work, but, if the United Nations organisation is turned into such an *agora*, these democracies would instinctively draw together and become, before long, a kind of united party. Though small, such a party would have a moral force out of all proportion to its

size, because its point of view would be evident and intelligible
and its objectives clear. If such a fundamentally different attitude
towards the United Nations were adopted the formation of
groups among the non-committed nations like the Afro-Asian
bloc would no longer be feared or even disliked. In fact the
presence of uncommitted nations would serve as a challenge,
because the battle for their allegiance would be fought out before
them between the democratic party and the monolithic Soviet
bloc. The evidence should be put before the world in the *agora*
and the world should be allowed to make its own decisions. In
this way the present jockeying for position and the undignified
canvassing for votes behind the scenes would be completely
eliminated, because there would be no need to secure a majority;
democracy's strength and its defensive power would not be
derived, even theoretically, from the United Nations. The
members of this 'democratic party' would accept the decisions taken by the majority of votes in all matters which did
not concern the defence of democracy itself. If decisions were
taken against the vital interests of the 'democratic party' the democratic countries would not be bound by them, because the West
would have served notice, well in advance, that in all matters
affecting the security of the democratic countries, it is determined
to take action by itself if necessary.

It is hardly yet recognised in the West how tragically and disas-
trously its reputation has sunk in the eyes of the non-committed
nations. The policy of misrepresentation, abuse and anti-Western
propaganda, practised by the communists for years past, has now
born fruit, particularly in Asia and Africa. As Walter Lippmann
pointed out, there is barely a country in which pro-Western
parties and pro-Western politicians are not today 'in trouble'.

To dispel the ill effects of this propaganda and to prove its good
faith the West must no longer assume that the moral basis of its
policy and position is self-evident. The West must draw upon its

true and profound resources and prove to the rest of the world that the democratic powers alone defend the rights of the individual against any *étatiste* political structure. A further minor advantage, which could be derived from such an attitude, should not be overlooked. If the struggle between communism and democracy were deliberately undertaken within the precincts of the United Nations *agora*, the present flagging interest in United Nations proceedings would give way to a red-hot watchfulness; the debates would be followed by the whole world, just as parliamentary debates are followed by the whole country.

Such a development must have a beneficial effect on the United Nations itself, giving it more vitality and power and greater resilience, since its existence would no longer depend on the unanimous support of the Great Powers.

It is a mistake to assume that all communist action derives from the quest for naked power. Undoubtedly this particular ingredient is very important in the communist make-up. Undoubtedly, naked power is exercised by communist parties *once they hold the reins of government*. Nevertheless, the would-be communist, in the free world at any rate, often embraces the new creed for higher motives. To gauge correctly the strength of communism it must be understood by the West that communist action often springs from a morality, less demanding than the morality of Western civilisation, but just as real and equally, if not more, binding in view of its more drastic and far more tangible sanctions. Once this truth is fully recognised by the West, democracy will have a real chance to repel the force of this new morality, for the simple reason that Western morality is infinitely superior to a morality which turns the communist into an effective political instrument.

The standards of behaviour in the communist world are set by an all-powerful state; the individual is cajoled or beaten into abiding by them. The strength of the West is derived from the individual. The action of the state is the expression of the sum total of all the individual wills which together form the will of the state. The standards of the West are constantly improving *pari passu* with the improvement of all individuals, a process still at work, as it has been for centuries past.

It has been argued that far too much emphasis is placed on presenting freedom as an ideal; that people who live on the brink of starvation are not interested in the ideal of freedom and cannot understand it. All they want to know is where their next meal will come from. This argument is largely correct. But what is the alternative? The West can either fight for the democratic ideal and educate the people to understand it through its success in practice, both at home and abroad, or embark upon an open competition of power politics with the Soviets. If the second course of action is chosen the West might still conceivably win. But by applying power politics to world affairs on a long-term basis the West is surrendering the fight. No one would deny that situations of imminent danger require from time to time 'strong' methods that are temporarily unavoidable. But, by playing power politics as a matter of principle, the West would sacrifice the very conception and ideal of democracy. It would sacrifice the moral strength of its cause. If such a course were charted, openly or pragmatically, the West would have on its side only the force of the arms which it can produce. The non-committed nations will not rally to the side of the West on those terms.

Colonel Nasser's decision, in July 1956, to nationalise the Suez Canal Company provides an apposite illustration to this point.

His action was undoubtedly high-handed. For months before he made that drastic decision, he played the East against the West in a profitable game closely resembling outright blackmail. Nasser also disregarded certain contractual obligations *vis-à-vis* the Suez Canal Company and abruptly terminated its concession which should have been operative for at least another eleven years.

The interest of the West in the freedom of passage through the Canal is undeniable. Over ninety per cent of Europe's oil, which is essential to Europe's industrial life, comes from the Middle East and most of it through the Suez Canal. West European trade with East Africa, South Asia and the Far East is important to both East and West. The closing of the Canal would sorely hit all interested countries, for the trip round the Cape adds from 2,000 to 5,000 miles to all the normal East-West trade routes, thereby considerably increasing the price of the commodities moved. Some experts go as far as to predict Europe's economic disaster in the event of the Canal's being closed. Although this last assertion is by no means justified, the world at large was aware of the issues at stake and of the extent to which Europe's interests were adversely affected by Nasser's unilateral action. Nevertheless the sympathy of the non-committed nations was with Nasser who managed to present his case as Egypt's struggle against the Anglo-French imperialists. When the use of force by Britain and France became a distinct possibility, wiser heads even in the West recoiled before the prospect. It was never denied that Britain and France were the injured parties; it was never doubted that they had a right to defend their interests, that they were right to prepare for military action at Suez, or even in Egypt, if Colonel Nasser were to close the Canal. But it was recognised that, so long as the freedom of passage through the Canal, as embodied in the 1888 Convention, remained unimpaired, any use of force by the Western Powers would amount to a step back into imperialism. If Britain were to impose her point of view by force of arms her claim to be the upholder of international law and morality would be gravely endangered if not utterly destroyed.

What are the Western interests affected by Colonel Nasser's move?

In the first place, there are the interests of the shareholders, most of whom are either Western co-operate bodies or Western individuals. But the right to nationalise is a purely domestic matter. It may be right or wrong to nationalise a particular industry, or a certain enterprise, but the decision is the sole right of the government of the day. The fact that certain, or all for that matter, of the shares are being held by non-nationals does not invalidate this right provided that fair compensation is offered to all the dispossessed foreign shareholders. This aspect of the problem was fully and dispassionately discussed in the progressive newspapers of the West. Among the non-committed nations the entire Press, as far as can be ascertained, was unanimous in fully supporting Nasser's right to nationalise an Egyptian Company and a Canal the entire length and all the installations of which were on Egyptian soil.

In the second place there are the interests of the users of the Canal. They need freedom of navigation without any discrimination, against payment of *fair* canal dues. Colonel Nasser fully realised the importance of keeping the Canal open and spared no effort or expense to ensure this in the months that followed the seizure.

Thirdly, there is need for the adequate upkeep of and improvements to the Canal installations, so that the ever-increasing number as well as size of ships using the Suez Canal, can be efficiently dealt with.

Finally, there was the Western fear that if Nasser 'got away with it' his example would be followed throughout the Middle East. At the height of the Suez crisis, it was argued that, unless a show of force were made and Nasser beaten to his knees, Middle Eastern oil would also be nationalised. The force of example is certainly great, but it would be nearer to reality to assume that Western participation in the oil industry of the Middle East is welcome only while Western capital and skill, particularly skill, are needed there. This is not a comforting thought for the West, but it is realistic. A sound long-term policy would be based on the idea that Western presence in the Middle East is only justified as long as it is wanted by the people of the Middle East. And Western presence will be wanted if it continues to be, as it is at present, beneficial to Middle Eastern interests. Nationalisation of the oil industry of that area will not be prevented by Western fear of it, nor by Western intention to deny to Middle Eastern governments the exercise of the right to nationalise.

Any interference with this right is power politics, however strong a case the West may have. The non-committed nations would resent it and the moral case of the West—as the upholder of international law and morality—would be destroyed.

By embarking upon a policy of power politics, whether open or concealed, the West will face alone, with no chance of gathering new allies, an expanding force which has a powerful, effective and appealing morality of its own—a force which is still making daily converts throughout the non-communist world. No argument as to the state of affairs in the countries already under communist rule will ever deter the dissatisfied in the non-communist world from embracing communism. The only way to prevent the gradual expansion of communist power is the provision by the West of a more potent moral power. This the West now possesses but refuses to use.

The only alternative open to the West, therefore, is to present the ideal of liberty as a worth-while objective to all the people of the world, especially to the illiterates who are now on the brink of starvation. The argument is not, of course, complete if presented like that. It is not the starving and illiterate people of the world who choose the path to be followed. They merely offer mass support to their leaders, and their leaders, we can rest assured, even in the most backward countries, are perfectly capable of understanding the meaning of liberty. They will decide for democracy and not for communism if they can see that democracy can offer a better life to their people.

The West must cease to pontificate. As Khrushchev and Bulganin were very quick to point out during their 1955 trip to South-East Asia, Western civilisation is relatively new. The people of Asia, particularly those of India and China, can boast of civilisations going back thousands of years before Western civilisation was born. The merits of the Western way of life may or may not seem attractive to the Asian leaders, but we can be certain that they are rightly proud of their own age-long traditions. Consequently the West must approach the non-committed nations with respect and accept their judgment about their own way of life. Only thus will the cause of the West, particularly in Asia, not be lost. Once the uncommitted nations truly believe that the West is ready to serve humanity rather than defend its selfish interests they will turn away from communism and believe the democratic way of life to be worth while. Though they may not have known parliamentary democracy and individual freedom, their civilisations are based on a far superior understanding of the internal freedom of the individual in communion with the forces of creation than the West has ever experienced, or, judging by all signs, is likely to experience in the years to come. Surely, this potent factor which opposes the Asian people in particular to communism should be working for democracy? Once they understand democracy they will realise that democracy, far from infringing upon that internal liberty of the individual which they cherish, merely enhances it and gives it full play, by producing an outward orderly society in which the physical expression of each individual life is guaranteed. They will realise that democratic institutions are merely there to serve them, to secure a more complete fulfilment of each individual life.

Can such a policy of open competition with communism for the allegiance of the uncommitted peoples of the world become a reality? Is it not Utopian to talk in terms of transforming the United Nations into a sort of parliament, however imperfect, where two parties, the democrats and the communists, would openly struggle for supremacy, and for capturing the support of the uncommitted members?

The answer to these questions is most emphatic. The conditions under which a parliament can function in a country are already present today on a world-wide scale. A parliament can function provided that any of the opposing parties are prevented from using force to acquire power. The development of nuclear weapons, the apocalyptic destruction which they can wreak on any concentrated objective in one stroke, the lack of effective means of detection or prevention, have brought about a *de facto* outlawing of world war. For fear of reprisals, if for no other reasons, no leaders in their senses could contemplate the unleashing of nuclear war. The territory from which nuclear weapons could be launched or carried is so vast that no potential aggressor could reasonably hope to destroy, in one initial sweep, an enemy's power of reprisal. The result is an armed deadlock, which prevents the outbreak of a world war almost as effectively as the existence of an international police force. Moreover, the latest developments in anti-tank warfare seem to suggest that the days of the big tanks are over; the accuracy of the latest missiles is so great and their destructive power so enormous, that it is reasonable to conclude that soon enough firing power will make a war of movement out of date. The world might well see itself in the next decade or two in a position which will make an armed invasion impossible, even on a small scale. If such an invasion were started effective means of stopping and repelling it could be rushed, with speed and efficiency, to the scene of battle.

In a democracy the open competition between two parties advocating diametrically opposed policies is not affected by minor skirmishes between their supporters in some distant constituencies.

The hot-heads responsible for the incidents are brought to book and the struggle for power goes on in an orderly, civilised way. The development of modern warfare brings about precisely this situation in the world at large. In the autumn of 1955 Khrushchev and Kaganovich stated quite plainly and publicly, from platforms separated in space by thousands of miles, that the 'socialist camp' is eager and ready to compete with capitalism, convinced that victory is theirs. At a banquet given in the Kremlin in honour of Mr. Kekkonen, the Finnish Prime Minister, Khrushchev said, with characteristic bluntness 'If you think your capitalistic system is capable of doing something, let us compete. We will show you.'

Let the West accept this challenge, because the conditions under which competition without war is possible are present. Once the concept of one world is jettisoned and the United Nations Organisation is turned by the West into what it should be, the West need not fear competing openly with communism. The West is fighting a losing battle only so long as its stand is confused and open to charges of insincerity and perfidy. But the West has not only the right and ability to enter successfully into competition with communism; it has a solemn duty and a grave responsibility before history to do so. This, the Western leaders cannot escape. Today, it is their duty to defend and further the rights which the individual has won against the state.

To enter into this competition effectively, however, the West must dispose of the dead wood which it has accumulated in the past. It must shed, in the first place, the methods of old-fashioned diplomacy, which no longer correspond to the needs of a changing world.

IV

NATIONALISM

IT has often been said, and certainly the communists would have us believe it, that the twentieth century is the age of communism, and it is true that the first half of the twentieth century has seen the rise and establishment of communist power. Historians of the future, however, may well pronounce the verdict that the twentieth century was the age in which nationalism made its most effective strides throughout the world. During the eighteenth and the nineteenth centuries the nation-state became a reality, but nationalism was effective only in Europe. Even in Europe the extension eastward of the nation-state principle was only achieved at the beginning of the twentieth century, after the formal proclamation that the national right to self-determination was available to all peoples made at the end of the First World War and enshrined in the famous Wilsonian principles. Viewed from a distance in time, the history of the first half of the twentieth century in Europe may well be described as the age in which nationalism was the most effective force, which led, not only to the re-drawing of Europe's map on national lines, but also to the inevitable excesses of extreme nationalism run wild, exploited by Fascism and Nazism. But these phenomena, which held the centre of the stage in the thirties and forties and temporarily obscured all else, were not the only notable developments of nationalism as a political force. Throughout the first half of the twentieth century nationalism and the nation-state idea, as conceived and practised in the West, gradually became a real force in the rest of the world, particularly in Asia. From the vantage-point of time, the future historian may well decide that the twentieth century interplay of real forces was characterised by the birth of national 'morale' in nations which had never understood it, in the Western sense, in all their history. Indian nationalism is a particularly apposite example.

Viewed in this light it seems correct to conclude that nationalism remains the most potent force of our age. In so far as it sways the non-white populations of the world, nationalism is a new force as well as a most powerful one. Non-white nationalism has gathered strength in the first half of this century, and now in the second proves to be capable of providing the reality upon which new, emergent states are being built. Communism catches the headlines today, because of its monolithic structure, its world-wide appeal and, more especially, because of the powerful direct challenge which it presents to Western democracy. However, in its struggle for world domination, communism gives ample evidence that it is fully aware that nationalism is the most powerful force in the world today. Where communism cannot deliberately use nationalism to serve its own purpose, it fights nationalism with all the means at its disposal.

By definition nationalism is a centrifugal, disparate force making for diversity in the world. Its basis is a corporate feeling of belonging to a group, tightly knit by common ties of language, past traditions and aspirations for the future. Communism recognises that this is the age in which nationalism makes its impact felt throughout the world outside Europe. It recognises that nationalism is fighting today to assert itself everywhere.

The communist approach to this force is twofold. Within the area 'liberated' by communism nationalism is brutally suppressed. Communists realise that nationalism is an ideological, spiritual force, far more powerful and real to human beings than communism. Any doubt as to the respect with which the Soviets regard the force of nationalism can be dispelled by the example of Stalin who revived an extreme nationalist spirit in Russia during his war against Hitler. Indeed, when Moscow was threatened and the German armies were pressing deep into the Caucasus, Stalin rallied the Soviet peoples, not to the defence of communism, but to the defence of 'Mother Russia'. The great military leaders of the Tzarist past were restored to glory overnight and placed on the roll of honour. The fight against the invader was a powerful nationalist fight for the defence of national existence. In retrospect, one can but wonder at Hitler's ineptitude in his treatment of the Byelo-Russian, Ukrainian and other under-privileged nations of the Soviet Union. Had he but recognised and acted upon the force of nationalism which inspired these peoples, instead of treating them as sub-human, the course of contemporary history might well have been different. At the end of the war, however, Stalin retraced his steps. The concessions made to nationalism in the thick of battle were withdrawn. Nationalist feelings were again forcibly directed into the artificially created 'Soviet patriotism'. All the communities which had shown unmistakable signs of nationalism when liberated from Moscow's rule, like the Kalmyks, Ingushi, and other Crimean Tartars, were bodily removed by Stalin from their homestead and scattered throughout the Soviet Union immediately after the war.

The communist attitude towards nationalism outside the Moscow-ruled world is one of uncanny understanding of the advantages which can be derived from it. The Indonesian Prime Minister, Mr. Harahap, speaks of unilateral abrogation by Indonesia of the Netherlands-Indonesia Union. The Cairo radio broadcasts daily with remarkable success in practically all the major languages of the African continent: Bari, Nuer, Shilluk, Zande, Dinka, Moru, Nuba, Hadendowa and Swahili, the *lingua franca* of many East African tribes, as well as Arabic. Countless other examples could be quoted to prove the reality of the nationalist force. The communist policy towards this force is one of active support, directing it against the West. At the same time it maintains that the Soviet Union is permeated through and through by a deep respect for all nationalities. In the Soviet-Afghan communiqué given at the end of the Soviet-Afghan talks in December 1955, for example, the second paragraph says:

'The Governments believe that nations and peoples at present deprived of freedom and sovereignty are entitled, according to the United Nations Charter, to determine their own future without restrictions or pressure.'

During their tour of South-East Asia the Soviet leaders played accurately upon the nationalist feelings of their hosts. In Rangoon, where they were met by a guard of honour giving the communist salute, they talked of Burma's greatness and Burma's cultural achievements. In New Delhi Krushchev quoted Lenin and associated India with Russia and China as the powers which would eventually determine the fate of the world. It is not surprising that Nehru himself warned his friends in the West that the 'time is past when the destinies of peoples can be decided by others. It is now the people of Asia who have to take their own decisions on matters concerning them'.

The West, on the other hand, has an extraordinary attitude towards nationalism. Instead of recognising it as the force most active in the world today, inspiring the allegiance of people everywhere, not only in their minds but in their hearts as well, the West prefers to ignore it or to oppose it. The situation is truly paradoxical. Nationalism is diametrically and irreconcilably opposed to communism. Nationalism is perfectly compatible with democracy. Yet, today, nationalism is communism's most effective ally in its uncompromising fight for the destruction of Western democracy.

The explanation for this terrible tragedy is largely historical.

Most progressive thinking in the democratic West fears nationalism for perfectly valid reasons. Rampant nationalism, particularly in Germany and to a lesser extent in Italy, has led to two great wars which have sapped Europe's power and taken away her world supremacy. Nationalism run wild has disastrous consequences. It exalts the nation-state, and it can lead, as it has done, to irrational excesses and catastrophe. Chauvinism is reactionary, dangerous, and its consequences can be terrible; a malignant growth which invariably spells the destruction of democratic liberties. The habit of equating nationalism with chauvinism is a hangover from the thirties, when we witnessed the emergence of extreme forms of nationalism in Europe, which resulted in untold suffering and destruction. But nationalism need never take this path. In its purest form nationalism is an utterly beneficial force. It is far more progressive than any of the pseudo-progressive forces which are usually, but unjustifiably considered to belong to the Left, for nationalism merely asserts the rights of all people to lead their own lives according to their own wishes, within the framework and limitations to their freedom set by the rules of behaviour of the comity of nations. Nationalism need never be aggressive. It only becomes so when the legitimate aspirations of a group are constantly denied by the Great Powers, or when nationalist feelings can be whipped up into a frenzy by unscrupulous power-seeking adventurers. In its truest essence the nature of nationalism has been expressed, with a masterly grasp, by Ion Codru-Dragusanu, a much-travelled Rumanian writer of the last century, who was steeped in Western culture, whilst always remaining an Easterner at heart. Here are his words:

'Many a time have I tried to penetrate the mystery of our warm feeling for our country, for our birthplace.

'He who never leaves his country has no idea what home means.

'You're born in a poverty-stricken village; brought up in a hut with a straw-thatched roof. You start binding together a few simple words. Sanda takes you in her arms. Ioana gives you an apple. Your Mother gives you a spanking. Your Father, a piggy-back ride. You forget it all and remember it all. You grow up. You get to know the vicarage and visit your aunts. New impressions, new knowledge.

'Then the cares and worries begin. You go to school in the next village. It's a long way off and the winter is rough. The first to greet you back is Giole the sheep-dog. I used to climb up the old hollow willow, at the far corner of the garden, and throw stones at the spruce by the front gate.

'I want to be back; with them, and for them.

'This is patriotism to me; both a reality and dream.'

This is the true meaning of nationalism. Its reality today is undeniable. The communist powers can use nationalism but in the long run cannot come to terms with it, since communism is the denial of nationalism. Communists can never hope to rally nationalism permanently to its side; by its very nature communism must seek the destruction of nationalism. Only democracy can successfully enrol nationalism on its side because there is no conflict between nationalism and democracy. In fact, nationalism can best prosper under the reign of democracy. They are born allies, as the very strong nationalism of the four component ethnical groups of Switzerland prove beyond any dispute.

The West should cease to fear nationalism. Orderly nationalism is a great power for good, and should be used by Western democracy as the main ingredient of a new, constructive world-wide policy. It is truly astounding that the West has so far tragically failed to recognise and enrol this remarkable force.

Today, the most powerful allies of the West are the peoples of Eastern Europe, who silently but staunchly refuse to be integrated into the system created by their Moscovite masters. Their effective passive resistance to communism is based almost entirely on nationalism. The peoples of Eastern Europe are the most truly reliable allies of Western democracy, since they have no misgivings about, and no fear of the West. They have only love and admiration for the free institutions which the West has brought into being. They have profound hatred for communism because, through their bitter experience, they have learnt what communism means.*

Yet these countries are utterly neglected. It is true that from time to time the Western leaders issue ringing pronouncements. In June 1954, President Eisenhower and Sir Winston Churchill declared: 'As regards formerly sovereign states now in bondage, we will not be a party to any arrangement or treaty which would confirm or prolong their subordination.' The same sentiments were expressed by President Eisenhower and Sir Anthony Eden in February 1956, when they declared: 'We shall help ourselves and our friends to peace, freedom and social progress, maintaining human rights where they are already secure, defending them when they are in peril and peacefully restoring them where they have temporarily been lost.' But such declarations do not amount to much. As Professor Salvador de Madariaga put it in a penetrating article entitled 'What the West is losing'[1] 'Nowhere in the West, not even in the most liberal papers in their most critical moments, does one read that such or such a proposal is to be rejected because it perpetrates the division of Europe. The division of Germany, yes. Everybody sees that it cannot be accepted. On the division of Europe silence all along the line.'

The sporadic espousing of the cause of the enslaved East European peoples has never led to practical policy. The Western Powers have never *demanded* of the Communist World to set its enslaved people free. Even when reference to their plight is

[1] *Manchester Guardian*, 14th November 1955.

made their cause is championed only by inference. All negotiations with the communist powers have been conducted so far under the appalling gloom engendered when East and West reach an agreement at the expense of these peoples. If only Russia would agree to the unification of Germany, European security might be accepted with the clear implication that the Eastern European peoples would be abandoned for good.

The force of nationalism outside Europe cannot yet be formally rallied to the side of democracy because nascent nationalism in the rest of the world finds itself in opposition to the Western Powers. To rally non-European nationalism under its flag democracy must give absolute proof of its good faith. It must show unmistakably that it is the friend of all the people who justifiably clamour for their independent national existence. The process of repairing their lost confidence and trust is a long and arduous one. But it is absolutely essential. It is a *sine qua non* of democracy's survival. To achieve this the West must remove all cause for suspicion of Western motives. It must transform the fear of European and American colonialism and imperialism into a relationship based on mutual trust. In the eyes of the colonial and semi-colonial people, as well as of the newly created independent countries, the Western democracies must become their powerful but trusted friends. For there is no other way. As long as the millions of uncommitted people do not regard the Western Powers as firm friends, careful of their susceptibilities and ready to serve their interests, the growing nationalism throughout the world outside Europe will inevitably turn to communism for the fulfilment of its hopes.

Footnote from p. 123.

* The statement contained in this paragraph would not have gone unchallenged before November 1956. The miraculous *nationalist* strength and bravery displayed by the Hungarian youth, supposedly communist indoctrinated, makes any further insistence on this point superfluous.

V

COLONIALISM AND IMPERIALISM

THE distinction between imperialism and colonialism is blurred. Colonialism is easy to define: all powers which have overseas dependencies, over which they rule, qualify for the name of Colonial Powers. Imperialism is etymologically derived from *imperium* or absolute power. Imperialist powers, therefore, must be those who have or seek absolute power over others. The two connotations apply to the same phenomenon. Imperialism, one may say, refers to its political aspect, whereas colonialism rather to its economic aspect. 'Old' imperialism is attributed to countries like Britain and France, which have had colonial empires in the past and continue to maintain them today. 'New' imperialism is attributed to those countries who are supposed to be seeking *imperium*—absolute power—over other countries. There is talk of dollar imperialism, which represents the unquestioned economic supremacy of the United States, and through which the Americans are supposed to be seeking domination over other countries. Such organisations as S.E.A.T.O. and M.E.T.O. are considered to be the disguise through which the 'new' imperialism finds its expression; it is asserted that the would-be imperialists are attempting through such agencies to regiment and dominate countries which are far from being the equals in strength of their initiators and main pillars.

Whatever the exact definition of these various terms, and whatever the exact nature and degree of control which the 'old' or 'new' imperialist and colonial powers seek to have over other peoples, the fact remains that it is a relationship between rulers and ruled, between powerful and weak, and between white and coloured. From the point of view of social dynamics, which is ultimately the subject-matter of politics, it is immaterial whether or not these hard-and-fast distinctions correspond to the truth. It is immaterial whether or not the charges against Western imperialism and colonialism are justified. The fact that the Western Powers are not seeking to establish a new form of imperialism is irrelevant to the present equation of power in South-East Asia so long as the people of South-East Asia think that they are.

There is no denying that the uncommitted nations, particularly in South-East Asia, are still very suspicious of Western motives. It is clear that the uncommitted nations throughout Asia and Africa still regard the white race, if not as a positive enemy, at any rate not as their trusted friends. They still distrust the objectives pursued by the West, when the West want them to collaborate in various schemes, such as S.E.A.T.O. or the Baghdad Pact. And, above all, the uncommitted nations are by no means convinced that the West is going to treat them on an equal footing, unaffected by any consideration of colour and race.

Upon this situation communist policy has played with consummate skill. The communist attacks on the West aim at conveying a very simple message:

(a) The Western Powers are the colonisers who hold down the people of Asia and Africa by naked or concealed, surreptitious force.

(b) The Western colonisers have interfered with the normal economic development of the countries of Asia and Africa and exploited them for their own selfish ends, and continue to do so where they can.

(c) The new imperialists, the United States and Britain, are trying to maintain their power by creating so-called defensive pacts.

126

In India in 1955, Bulganin made this last point very clearly by saying: 'These military groupings are causing suspicion among the people of Asia because the initiators of these pacts were in the past fighting on the side of the colonial powers.' The reaction was almost instantaneous. One of the most important Indian newspapers wrote: 'Colonialism has been taking a new and more dangerous form. The Baghdad Pact is a very dangerous trap laid by the Western nations.' (*Umrita Bazaar Patrika.*)

It is significant that Krushchev went even further, and pressed his advantage home by dissociating the white rulers of the Soviet Union from the rest of the white race: 'As a representative European nation we are ashamed of what those other Europeans did here before. But not all Europeans think as the colonisers did.'

The influence of Bandung cannot be overestimated. Trained observers like Vernon Bartlett see how the communist powers are making tremendous strides in Asia. In the eyes of the people of South-East Asia, who by tradition and instinct reject war and violence, the communist powers appear as the *upholders of peace*. The fact that so far the only victims of nuclear explosions have been Asians, at the hands of the Western Powers, is also having its effect.

The communist powers have also succeeded in convincing the uncommitted nations of Asia that *communism alone can tackle the problems of mass poverty*.

On both these counts the peoples of South-East Asia are so impressed that they completely overlook the drastic methods by which the communists achieve their ends. It is clear from the pronouncements of the Soviet leaders, at the 20th Congress of the Russian Communist Party in 1956, that the advantages already gained among the uncommitted nations would be pressed forward. Molotov ate humble-pie and confessed his Ministry's failure to make full use of the enormous possibilities 'offered by the unprecedented upsurge of the liberation struggle of the colonial and independent peoples.'

One of the lines along which the communists mean to destroy Western influence in the uncommitted countries is by stressing the importance of equating economic with political independence. This means, in effect, that, so long as the Western Powers still have great economic interests in their newly created independent states, true political independence is not achieved. The presentation of the problem in this way instantly appeals to the subconscious mind of all Indians or Burmese who still distrust the vast Western economic interests. Though loyal to the present governments, these continue to be controlled by people in Europe or America.

The problem facing the West in this field is enormous. Outright foes, indifferent bystanders, or suspicious would-be friends, who admire many things Western, must be turned into firm friends. A bold approach, on a vast scale, must be the fountainhead of a new, far-reaching, long-term Western policy. In Vernon Bartlett's words, 'the change in the world balance of power since the Bandung Conference, in April 1955, calls for a re-examination of Western policy in comparison with which Mr. Dulles's agonising "re-appraisal" of a few years ago was an infantile exercise.'

The problem is of the utmost urgency. If the bold new policy required is not at once put into the workshops of the Foreign Office and the State Department, tomorrow it may be too late. The signs are unmistakable. Nascent Asian and African nationalism is on the march. It is no longer overawed by the Western Powers, as was proved by its ability to mobilise sufficient support to out-vote the 'colonial powers' and their supporters on the question of Algeria at the United Nations. In Rome, in November 1955, to quote another example, Britain was unseated from the Executive Council of the United Nations Food and Agriculture Organisation, although Britain is the world's biggest importer of wheat. All who attended the Conference are certain that this move was proof not only of the uncommitted nations' desire for self-assertion but also of an act of malice against the so far unchallenged 'colonial powers'.

It would be hopeless to try to reverse this powerful trend, which will doubtless gather momentum if the leaders of the Western world continue to associate themselves with, or to endorse, doubtful moves. The British-Australian-Dutch proposal at the United Nations Social Committee is a relevant example. These powers suggested that the first article of the draft covenants on human rights should be struck out. This article states:

(1) All peoples shall have the right to freely determine their political, social, economic and cultural status.

(2) All nations administering territories shall promote the realisation of this right.

(3) The right of self-determination includes permanent sovereignty over natural wealth and resources.

This article fully recognises the right of all peoples to aspire to an independent national life and to exploit for their own benefit the wealth that nature has bestowed upon them. It is not only legitimate but also desirable that the people of the world should know that they can pursue their own happiness in their own way with the fullest support of the Western Powers. In fact it is essential that they should be fully convinced that the West is the staunchest upholder of their rights.

No one in his senses would belittle the vastness of the problem. But it is today that its solution must be found. Western action must be guided by a policy directly aimed at (a) satisfying the national aspirations of all colonial, semi-colonial and under-privileged nations throughout the world, and (b) removing the taint of racialism which still lingers on and is still associated with the Western Powers. No one who has followed closely Britain's colonial policy since the war, can deny that Britain has pursued an enlightened course of action. Yet the fact remains that it has been in the nature of a rear-guard action. Concessions have been obtained through struggle, and independence has been wrested from Britain. The most recent developments show an even bolder approach. Both in the case of Malaya and the Caribbean, Britain has set out a pattern, one could almost say, 'ahead of time' if judged by previous standards, for the complete fulfilment of the national aspirations of the peoples concerned. But is even this enough? Does this mean that colonialism and imperialism have been rejected by the Western Powers?

The picture in Africa is hazy. The prospects of self-government are clear only in isolated cases. White supremacy is still a slogan which the communists can use effectively to bludgeon the Western powers. The French continue to ignore the temper of French Black Africa. Their policy seems to be based on the assumption that the whole vast area south of the Sahara is a quiet pond unrippled by the violent disturbances north of it. Portugal and Belgium have hardly had a colonial policy in keeping with the signs of the time. They concentrate on raising the standards of living of the native population by means of an efficient paternalist colonial administration. A sound policy, as far as it goes; but is it enough? The 16 million United States Negroes reputedly have an aggregate income of $16,000 million which is almost as much as the total income of 'prosperous Canada's 15·7 million citizens'.[1] But their material prosperity merely increases the urgency and insistence of their demands for the removal of segregation.

The white-black race relationship is far from satisfactory. Viewed as a world problem it was poignantly summed up by the Chief Minister of Bombay in the words: 'We are black and they are white.'

[1] See *Time*, 26th March, 1956.

Race relationship is an acute problem of permanent world-wide, significance. The attempt to solve it must be of equally vast proportions. The present trend is decidedly anti-Western, anti-white. In order to reverse this trend, the West must lay the foundation stone of a new world edifice inhabited equally by white and coloured alike.

The only way in which this state of affairs can be brought about, by which the white man can become the trusted elder of his black and yellow brother, is by a final declaration of policy on the part of all colonial powers to put an end to imperialism and colonialism in an orderly, well-defined and easily discernible way. A plan must be set out, in unmistakable language, which will define the conditions for achieving independence by stages. This clear-cut pattern of advancement should be open to all. Local conditions should obviously be taken fully into consideration, but, provided a certain stage of development is reached and certain conditions for admittance fulfilled, any nation in the colonial empire of the West should automatically have the right to claim an advance towards self-government. It will be said that the problem is far too intricate, the conditions far too diverse in the various colonial countries now under Western rule, and the stages of development of the colonial people so profoundly different from area to area, or even within one and the same geographical region, that an over-all plan cannot be worked out. New tribalism in Africa, the problems of the overcrowded African towns compared with the country districts, the need to safeguard the interests of the minority groups when the power is handed over . . . and so forth. These problems are real, but they do not invalidate the absolute need and the possibility of drawing up a master plan for an orderly progress by stages towards self-government, a master plan which would be available to all.

In the second place, it will be argued that the colonial powers each have different policies and different problems in their own colonies. Portugal's policy in Goa, France's policy in Ubangui-Shari, Holland's attitude towards New Guinea, or Belgium's Congo problems are so diverse that there is no common denominator. The same type of argument could have been and probably was advanced when the leaders of Western civilisation took drastic but determined and final steps, at the beginning of the last century, to end the slave trade. The end of colonialism will undoubtedly go against the material interests of the Western Powers. It will affect to a large extent the fortunes of those who have a great deal of capital invested overseas. But a bold, all-out attempt to remove the stigma of colonialism, to reject the charge of exploiting other people for selfish Western interests, must be made to-day, however much it might cost the West in terms of finance and material wellbeing. Otherwise, within a generation or two, the entire non-white world will become the sworn enemy of the West. The complete banning of the slave trade sorely hit many 'respectable' Western interests but by the end of the eighteenth century the conscience of the West could no longer countenance the continuance of this trade, and demanded that an end be put to it.

Slave traffic had been feared and abhorred long before the day it was finally discontinued, by the black peoples of whom thousands upon thousands were forcibly removed across the ocean. Colonialism is equally abhorred today by the colonial peoples. It is essential that the conscience of the West should finally recognise that colonialism must be ended. Unless colonialism is ended in an orderly fashion, unless the temper of the colonial peoples is recognised and the West stands by their side as friends and helpers, the West has no alternative but to continue to hold by force every colony until it has to be given up as a result of an open clash, which can only result in the fierce enmity of the colonial people concerned. If some 130 years ago the leaders of

the civilised world were capable of drawing up and then gradually
enforce a declaration for ending the slave trade,* so can the colonial
powers today, *mutatis mutandis*, produce a blue-print for ending
colonialism. This comparison between the slave-trade and colonialism will be strongly resented in many 'progressive' as well as
reactionary quarters. It is readily granted that the degree of exploitation exercised by the slave-owner is in no way comparable
to that derived by the coloniser from administering overseas lands.
But what is the civilising process unless our conscience gradually becomes more and more readily aroused in face of cruelty
and injustice? A conference of all colonial powers could be con-
vened and a plan agreed upon, setting out the stages which colonial development must follow in order to bring it to an end
by gradual, constitutional reform. The Western colonial powers
could then pledge themselves to allow all their subject people to
benefit from the plan and advance to a status of full independence
provided they earn and deserve it.

The advantages of such a course of action are incalculable.
Once a declaration is made and solemnly signed by all colonial
powers without exception it becomes binding in international
law. There could be no question of the Western colonial powers'
refusing to grant such advancement as is rightly claimed. And
the onus of proof would automatically pass from the Western
Powers, who today have to justify their reluctance to accord new
rights to any clamouring demagogue, to those who want more
freedom. Today, any irresponsible political hothead can whip up
anti-white feeling in some distant colony, create disturbances and
'prove', through violence, that his people want and deserve self-
determination. Though the colonial power can be perfectly
aware that the clamour for independence is lacking in genuine
popular support, and convinced that the demand for independence
is unjustified and, if granted, would lead to the assumption of
power and the oppression of other groups by a small, irresponsible

133

group, yet the colonial power is hard put to prove its case before the unforgiving tribunal of world opinion. It is in the unenviable position of having to choose between prematurely granting independence, and thus creating new and greater local problems, and appearing ruthless, reactionary and selfish.

If, however, a blue-print for gradual advancement has become international law it will be the task of those demanding a further advance in their national status to prove that conditions qualifying them for greater independence exist in their particular land. There would be no danger at all of granting further advancement prematurely, and no stigma attached to a refusal by the colonial power. On the contrary, the colonial power, abiding by the solemn contract which it will have signed, will serve the interests and earn the respect, even love, of all colonial peoples. Violent upheavals would largely be frustrated. Concessions would no longer be grabbed by force, they would be earned. Democracy would no longer be fighting a rear-guard action in the colonies. Advancement for colonial peoples would be an orderly change in an orderly society. In the eyes of the colonial people, democracy would be restored to its true position. Democracy would be for them the best safeguard of their own interests—of the interests of each member of today's colonial community throughout the world. Democracy would become, what it must become for them, an ideal, and the only ideal, towards which it is worth striving. Such a declaration by all colonial powers would largely remove the taint of racialism which is still attached to the Western Powers. Then, the present colonial and coloured peoples of the world could accept Western friendship without any arrière-pensée.

A recent development in the right direction is the formation, in 1956, of a non-racial political party in Tanganyika, pledged to work for the political and social integration of all races in the country. This party has been heralded as the first truly multi-

racial party enjoying a virtual control in any of the colonial legis-
latures. For the first time, racialism has been totally rejected by
the party in power. This is the line of development which bodes
well for the future. Its impact upon the minds of the coloured
people is far greater than countless high-sounding Western
proclamations.

Footnote from p. 133.

* The Emancipation Act, 1833, led to the release of all slaves in the British
Empire by 1840. Slavery was ended by France in 1848, by Holland in 1863
and by the United States in 1865.

VI

DEFENSIVE SYSTEMS

THE Western policy of military alliances, pacts and treaties is in sore need of re-examination and revision. It has already been indicated that this policy has led to widespread, almost violent criticism from many quarters. It has already been shown that the value of many of the military pacts and defensive alliances is doubtful. The problem needs further elucidation.

A look at the map of the world is sufficient to explain the purpose of these military agreements. N.A.T.O. brings together the countries of North America and practically the whole of Western Europe, stretching into Greece and Turkey in the Eastern Mediterranean. M.E.T.O. purports to unite Turkey, Iraq, Persia and Pakistan. S.E.A.T.O. links together Pakistan, Thailand and the Philippines, as well as the Western Powers and the British Dominions in the Southern Hemisphere. Military alliances and friendship pacts, as well as direct military support, bind the United States to the Chinese nationalists on Formosa, the Diem régime in South Vietnam, Syngman Rhee's South Korean State and Japan. The objective is quite clear. The Western Powers have tried to create a chain of defensive systems capable of offering security to all the countries round the borders of the communist-dominated world. They are strictly defensive in nature. They represent a perfectly legitimate and justifiable desire to prevent a further communist expansion either by invasion or by an internal *coup d'état* lacking popular support.

Chronologically, the first of these defensive systems is the North Atlantic Treaty Organisation. Many criticisms can be levelled against it; nevertheless N.A.T.O. can be considered a success. All countries embraced by it are democracies in various stages of development, but the parliamentary system of government secures a continuity of foreign policy and therefore guarantees continued membership of the organisation no matter what governmental changes may take place. Even such difficulties as the Greek-British and Greek-Turkish conflict over Cyprus cannot disturb the existence of the pact, for the simple reason that all its members, no matter what clash of immediate interests there may be between them, are determined to safeguard and defend their free institutions and prevent the establishment of communist dictatorship in their countries. They realise that by remaining united in their common determination the effectiveness of the resistance which they can offer communist aggression and subversion is greater than the sum total of their actual defensive forces.

The military leaders of the West have frequently pointed out that the budgetary effort made by the member countries of N.A.T.O. and the deployment of forces in Europe, where the danger of a possible communist aggression is always present, is far from sufficient to meet locally a communist armed attack. In the various discussions round the problem of using tactical atomic weapons for a limited war, it is also pointed out that, to redress the required equilibrium in Europe between the communist forces under arms in their European Command and those of N.A.T.O., atomic missiles of all descriptions must be used. In 1956, Marshal Zhukov gave stern warning—which the Soviets may or may not mean in all seriousness—that should the Western Powers use any atomic weapon, however limited in radius of destructiveness, and even if only for tactical purposes, the Soviet Union would embark upon a total atomic war directed at the heart of the capitalist world, at the great American cities in the United States. Be this as it may, the fact remains that the stockpile of nuclear bombs in the United States and Britain is so great, and the means of delivering them so efficient, that it is clear that no war could be started in Europe by the Soviet Union without dire risks to herself. Thus, in spite of its many shortcomings, the high command of the N.A.T.O. forces can claim to be in control of the situation and capable of deterring Soviet aggression in Europe. But the main strength of N.A.T.O. is not so much its military, actual or potential force, but rather the will which animates all the like-minded nations who have appended their signatures to the Paris Agreements.

The same cannot be said of the other defensive systems obviously created on the pattern of N.A.T.O. Again in chronological order, the creation of S.E.A.T.O. was by all standards a singularly unsuccessful, if not altogether abortive, attempt to unite the nations of South-East Asia in a defensive alliance.

No defensive organisation can claim to unite the people of South-East Asia, if such important countries as India, Burma and Indonesia are left out. The proposal for the creation of S.E.A.T.O., and the way in which it was presented to the people of South-East Asia, cannot therefore be considered well-timed or well prepared.

The same applies to the Middle East Treaty Organisation. Born of the Turkish-Iraqi defensive pact by the adherence of Iran and Britain, M.E.T.O. was intended by the planners to bring into one defensive system all the countries of the Middle East. The formal invitation addressed to Jordan only led to riots and the fall of the Jordanian government. Egypt, Saudi Arabia, Syria, and even Lebanon but to a lesser extent, declared their enmity to this pact, and stayed out of it.

The first question must therefore be: are such pacts of any permanent value, if they leave out important, if not overwhelmingly important areas, whose defence they are supposed to serve? The answer is open to argument. But there is far more to it.

In almost every case, these defensive organisations in South-East Asia and the Middle East have been concluded with totalitarian governments whose tenure of office is more often than not dependent upon their ability to maintain themselves in power through the control of the police and of the armed forces, even against open opposition, and almost always against a background of passivity, backwardness and lack of concern over public affairs. Trained observers now reporting the situation in the member countries of these two defensive systems, are agreed, without a single dissenting voice, that the populations concerned know nothing of the existence of these pacts, or, if they have heard of them, are distrustful or uninterested in them, or else openly and violently opposed to them.

The defensive system, therefore, is created in both these areas solely with the concurrence of the governments in power. This leaves the door wide open to criticism from within. The fall of the Jordanian Government should be a warning. Furthermore, far from inculcating the democracy which they preach for themselves, the senior Western Powers bolster up these totalitarian régimes by concluding such pacts with them. The wisdom of doing this is doubtful, to say the least. Besides, not being based on a broad, popular support the governments in power, signatories of the defensive systems created at Western behest, may change their policy overnight and keep for their own purposes the armaments poured into their countries by the West.

This point can best be illustrated by the strange experiment the West encouraged when it was thought that Tito might be won for the West. Tito's quarrel with the Cominform in 1948 led to a chain of events. Economic aid and full political support were given to the communist dictator. Later, the formation of a Balkan Pact between Yugoslavia, Greece and Turkey was encouraged. State visits were exchanged between the communist dictator and his new-found allies. Western diplomacy seemed to be successful.

But Stalin died. The new leaders in the Kremlin went to Belgrade with sackcloth and ashes and embraced the lost friend. Less and less was heard of the Balkan Pact. After the Summit Geneva meeting Tito made a broadcast in which he boldly stated that the military aspect of the Balkan Treaty had now a secondary character and that it would be against Yugoslav policy to strengthen this military pact. During the second Foreign Ministers' Geneva Conference in the autumn of 1955 the American Secretary of State, on a flying visit to Belgrade, paid his respects to the communist dictator. It was reported that the object of the visit was to hammer out a common Western policy towards the satellites. He was met with a flat refusal. The postscript to the whole Balkan Pact adventure is contained in Marshal Tito's letter of greetings to the 20th Congress of the Soviet Communist Party. He ranged his country with Russia among the progressive forces on which alone peace depends. Tito's visit to the Soviet Union in June 1956 was a triumphal march. Vast crowds mobbed him everywhere he went. 'I feel at home in the Soviet Union,' he said at the Black Sea resort of Sochi, 'because we are part of the same family, the family of Socialism.' At the end of his stay, after signing the joint communiqué, Marshal Zhukov removed the last vestige of a doubt as to where Tito now stands. He said: 'If a war is imposed on us we will fight together, shoulder to shoulder, as in the last war for the happiness of mankind.' Tito's 're-defection' was complete, to the consternation of the Western Powers. Yet there is nothing surprising about it. Tito always spoke and acted like a communist. His quarrel was with Stalin, not with communism. Had he been accepted by Stalin as an equal, as he was accepted by the Kremlin, during 1955–56, the 1948 split would never have occurred. If Moscow continues to treat him as an equal partner, leaving him the undisputed master of his own communist country, Tito will continue to be a loyal member of the communist fold.*

Pakistan, to quote another example, has always been represented as being one of the staunchest supporters of S.E.A.T.O. Arms have been delivered to Pakistan in such quantities that, according to Indian spokesmen, the balance of forces between India and Pakistan is today disturbed. Deeply concerned over the explosive Kashmir conflict, the Indian leaders have frequently protested against this with unusual vehemence. The Indian charges may or may not be justified. But Pakistan's inclusion in S.E.A.T.O. has also led to Russia's taking a direct interest in Pakistan. To mark the importance which the Soviets accord to the establishment of 'good' relations even with such countries as Pakistan, who frequently demonstrate their friendly attitude towards the West and openly proclaim their desire to advance steadily towards a fully democratic form of government, Moscow has sent no less a representative than Anastase Mikoyan to attend the festivities celebrating Pakistan's full independence and republican status. The Soviet purpose is clear. They want the disruption and destruction of all defensive systems. If threats that Pakistan is playing the imperialist game, emanating from New Delhi and Khabul, do not yield results, Russia is ready to make friendly overtures to Pakistan, offering 'relations with Pakistan no less friendly than those with India', and hinting at important economic aid. There is no suggestion as yet that Pakistan will take the course of other countries who have successfully played the West and East against each other for their immediate material benefit, but the possibility must not be excluded. Such partners in these defensive systems are therefore doubtfully reliable.

The N.A.T.O. Pact contains important economic provisions and the wealth made available to those partners who needed it most in order to stabilise and strengthen their economies has been very effective. The S.E.A.T.O. and the M.E.T.O. defensive systems also contain such provisions. The approach, therefore, is similar, but the situation is fundamentally different. In the case of N.A.T.O., the signatories are united by a common bond of belief in democracy. They would have signed a defensive alliance whether economic aid was forthcoming or not, because democracy was threatened. In the case of S.E.A.T.O. and M.E.T.O., America and Britain offered armaments and economic help, in various guises, and it is largely the prospect of this economic help which often swung the balance in favour of joining the Pact. The morality of such economic 'incentives' is doubtful. They amount to a form of blackmail which produces no genuine affection and response, but only contempt and resentment, because it derives, itself, from contempt. These incentives are offered on the assumption that the conscience can be bought, that the weaker partner can be made to accept a military alliance, for which it has no particular love, for the sake of material benefits. The American motives are admirable and their determination to stop communism serves the interest of the whole world. Their performance in offering vast sums of money to other countries is without precedent in history. Yet one should not ignore reality. This enormous 'aid' has only succeeded in creating throughout Asia a virulent, widespread resentment. So much so, that one of the most pro-American British correspondents in the Far East reported early in 1956 that the Americans are the most hated people throughout Asia. The cause of this outburst of feeling is unmistakable. The people of Asia are aware that this 'aid' is not so much pro-Asian as anti-communist. They are not interested in anti-communism as such. They are very much interested in economic assistance. They welcome it with open arms, but they want it without strings.

On all counts, therefore, the creation of military defensive systems is useless in areas which have no particular addiction to democracy. In the first place, they cannot align all the powers who matter in that area. Secondly, pacts are concluded at the top with the governments in power whose future conduct must remain essentially unpredictable. Thirdly, they lead to widespread resentment against, if not outright hatred of the democratic powers.

What, then, is left to justify the creation of such defensive systems? The answer must be their military effectiveness. On the best authority available—that of General Gruenther the former Head of N.A.T.O., the most efficient and most tightly knit defensive organisation of all such systems—we can say without hesitation that these defensive alliances are by themselves incapable of dealing with a direct communist attack. In the case of the S.E.A.T.O. Pact there is no provision for automatic action in case of communist aggression or subversion. It merely provides for instant consultations about the action to be taken. The corresponding clause in the M.E.T.O. Pact is even less stringent. The conclusion is inescapable. No one can claim that these pacts by themselves make for local security against communist attack.

It may be argued, however, that these pacts, even if not effective in themselves, provide a contractual obligation which in case of attack could serve as the basis for Western intervention in the territory of the victim country. Even this argument hardly holds water. Take the Baghdad Pact as an example. Already the Soviet Union attacks it as aggressive and hints that it might call into force those clauses of the 1921 Soviet-Persian Agreement which permits the Soviet Union to occupy North Iran in case aggression against the Soviet Union is prepared on Iranian soil. The conclusion of the M.E.T.O. Pact, therefore, gave the Soviets an excuse to claim interference in the internal affairs of some of the countries concerned.

Given Western determination to prevent the further spread of communism by open aggression, or by an attempt to capture power from within, any of the countries adjacent to the Communist World, when threatened directly, will appeal to the West for help. The Western Powers will surely find a way of either giving immediate military assistance to the threatened country, or of facing the nerve centres of communist power with the prospect of direct and unlimited war against themselves.

The argument here put forward should not be misunderstood. Military defensive systems are greatly to be welcomed. They serve as important stabilising factors. They convey to the people a sense of security derived from the knowledge that important world powers are ready to support them, arms in hand, in case of need. But such military systems are only valuable in so far as they correspond to the true wishes of the people they aim to support. The defensive system of the North Atlantic is completely beneficial, springing from realities. Similar defensive systems are highly desirable in the other areas of the world which are now threatened by communist expansion. But the systems which have been created so far in these areas have failed in their purpose. They must be re-examined and reformed not by patching them up, as the British Foreign Secretary suggested in the case of the M.E.T.O. Pact by reinforcing it through a Baghdad Plan on parallel lines to the highly successful Colombo Plan. If that were done, without a fundamental change in the approach towards those areas, such eleventh-hour expedients would merely lose their own intrinsic worth because they would inevitably be associated, in the minds of all critical observers, with the defensive anti-communist military alliances which they are meant to bolster up.

Footnote from p. 140.

* Far too much has been made of Tito's new disagreements with the Kremlin and of his flying visit to Crimea in the autumn of 1956. Tito left no doubt about his stand when he approved, in November 1956, the brutal Soviet suppression of the Hungarian revolution. If the Soviet leaders deny Tito the right to apply Marxism-Leninism in Yugoslavia in his own way, as the 'secret' Moscow circular letter of the summer of 1956 seems to suggest, then a new rift might become unavoidable, otherwise not.

VII

NEUTRALITY

AT this particular point of history, the main ingredient of a successful Western policy is sincerity. The Western Powers must convince the people of the world that their declared policy, of upholding the ideal of liberty for all people, strictly corresponds with their intentions. They must prove that they mean to translate their intentions into reality. Their actions must be fully consistent. It is not enough for the West to declare their fundamental opposition to communism, to draw all the logical conclusions from that opposition by rejecting the one-world-united-for-peace idea, and by putting the United Nations to a different use. It is not enough for the West to desist from an antiquated approach to foreign policy and diplomacy which leads to the conclusion of treaties and alliances at the top only, bereft of any popular support in the nations concerned. It is also necessary that the respect which the West has for the countries in the uncommitted world should be proved beyond any doubt. This does not mean only equality of treatment to be accorded to all nations. It also means, in practice, genuine respect for neutrality. Any pressure that the Western Powers bring to bear upon the countries who have decided to maintain an attitude of neutrality in the present world-wide struggle between communism and democracy will merely lead to a greater resistance on their part to Western advances. Pressure will also bring disrepute to the proclaimed ideals of the West, for love of freedom is not compatible with interference in other peoples' affairs.

Neutrality today is of different shades. There is the neutrality of Switzerland, going way back in history, which cannot permit the acceptance of any form of preferential international obligation to any state or group of states. But Switzerland is a functioning democracy. Her allegiance to Western democratic ideals is beyond question. A slightly less stringent type of neutrality is that of Austria. At its origin this neutrality was the price which the Austrian people had to pay for the unification of their country and the withdrawal of the Soviet troops from its Eastern Zone. This neutrality was born of an act of will imposed from outside on the people of Austria. Nevertheless, there are signs which justify the belief that neutrality is welcomed today by a large majority of the Austrian people. The constitutional law on perpetual neutrality specifically declares that of her own free will Austria 'will in future join no military alliances and will not permit the establishment of military bases of foreign states on her territory'. However, this type of neutrality does not prevent Austria from joining such organisations as the Council of Europe.

Swedish neutrality is a self-chosen path to avoid participation in any international organisations which could involve military or political commitments.

This type of neutrality, of which the three cases quoted are well-known examples, has one main common characteristic. They all abide by the democratic process of government. In the ideological struggle with communism they are all completely on the side of the West.

There is a different type of neutrality which has emerged because of, and during the present cold war. This neutrality, as practised by Colonel Nasser's Egyptian Government, has been labelled 'positive neutralism'. A military dictatorship by nature, this government seeks to maintain an equi-distant position between the two power blocs. In view of its important strategic and political position Egypt's friendship and alignment is desirable to both blocs. Hence Nasser's ability to play them against each other for his country's immediate benefit. His attitude to communism, though no democrat at heart, should be one of complete opposition. His opposition to the democratic West, though no communist, is more emotional perhaps, but equally final.

At the other end of the scale is the neutralism exemplified by Nehru's India. Nehru defined it as follows.

'We look forward to fruitful co-operation in the cause of peace and human welfare. Thus, friendship and co-operation are not competing against any nation or people. We hope the area of friendship and co-operation will be enlarged until it ultimately embraces the whole world. To that we dedicate ourselves.

'It is in no spirit of pride or arrogance that we pursue our own independent policy. We would not do otherwise unless we were false to everything India has stood for in the past and stands for today. We welcome association and friendship with all, and the flow of thoughts and ideas of all kinds, but we reserve the right to choose our own path.'

Parliamentary democracy functions in India today. Discussion can be taken through all the classic stages before it finally emerges into the law of the land, through parliament, which is the essence of democracy. Nevertheless, democracy is yet very imperfect in India. But since government by discussion is a reality and the establishment of democracy is the avowed purpose of the present-day Indian leaders, the future of Indian democracy can be viewed with some confidence. The Indian leaders are doing their utmost to perfect it by all the means at their disposal. In the struggle between communism and democracy Nehru has chosen to maintain a position of strict neutrality. In this, he seems to have the overwhelming support of his people, not only because of the great prestige which he himself enjoys but also because in its present mood India has no fear of communism.

Nehru seems to believe that up to the Geneva meeting on Indo-China the communist powers pursued an expansionist, aggressive policy. July 1954, according to Nehru, marks a significant turning point in history, for at that conference an armed conflict was ended, and an explosive situation was resolved, by negotiation and agreement. Up to that date, in Mr. Nehru's view, the organising of defensive security systems was justified. He understands and seems to accept the reasons which led to the creation of N.A.T.O. After that date, however, peaceful co-existence, particularly in Asia, which is his main concern, might have become a reality had it not been for the creation of S.E.A.T.O. and later of M.E.T.O. Nehru believes that both these pacts, which incidentally encircle India, ran counter to the atmosphere engendered by the July 1954 Geneva meeting. It is therefore Western action that increased tension in Asia without any real advantage to the West. Though not opposed to N.A.T.O. as such, he has a grudge against it because he feels that, through Portugal's membership, N.A.T.O. stretches a long arm into Goa.

By its very nature the Communist World threatens the existence of all non-communist governments. Neutralism is no shield against communist subversion, nor against a potential communist bid for power. Should the communist centres of power consider the situation and circumstances to be favourable and propitious, a bid for power will be made whether the would-be victim happens to be opposed to communism, or a staunch upholder of neutrality. There can be little doubt that the free world would best defend itself against communism if it were united without exception in total opposition to communism. But the West, in keeping with the very principles by which it lives, can never use stronger methods than peaceful persuasion. The West could, and should, point out on all possible occasions the danger of neutralism to the states and governments who have chosen it, as well as to the whole free world. But the allegiance which the West wants, and which is of value to the cause of democracy, must be freely given. Any coercion, however mild and innocuous, will destroy the very object which democracy tries to uphold in the face of the communist challenge.

We live in an age in which democracy and communism are in open competition for the support and friendship of all uncommitted nations. It is fallacious, and extremely dangerous, to maintain that the uncommitted nations do not understand the real issues at stake, or the nature of the struggle, and are ignorant of the danger under which they live. Such thinking merely leads to a paternalist policy on a world scale. It rests on the assumption that the uncommitted nations do not know what is good for them. This may largely be justified, in many countries; yet the West can never demand that their advice should be accepted.

A policy that will in the end inevitably draw the uncommitted nations to the side of Western democracy must begin by stressing, at every point, that the West is ready to defend any country who wishes to be defended against communist aggression, no matter in what form the communist bid for power is made. This tantamount to accepting a unilateral obligation to defend any country's independence. At present there are many countries among the uncommitted nations who do not believe that they are threatened by communist aggression. They consider any suggestion of a military or political alliance, for the purpose of preventing or repelling such a 'non-existent' threat, as an unwarranted interference in their internal affairs. This unilateral, contractual obligation, if freely undertaken by the great democracies of the West, with no corresponding commitments whatever on the side of the potential recipient, will ring true in the ears of the leaders of the uncommitted countries. In time they will believe in the sincerity of the West and will appeal for Western help if and when such help is required. But this feeling of confidence and trust in the sincerity of Western purpose will never be achieved unless the West has a profound and unquestioning respect for every country's right to choose neutrality if it so pleases.

Such a policy of respect for neutrality is perfectly consistent with the reality of the world situation today. As we have already stressed, the world today is divided into two fundamentally opposed camps: the Communist World, and those democratic countries who see the communist danger and are ready to unite in order to defend their free institutions against this threat. The rest of the world is made up of democracies at various stages of development and of totalitarian countries of different hues, which prefer to remain uncommitted. But they would swing to one or other of these powerful polarising centres, according to which of them promises more security, more material benefit, and more respect for their independent national existences. Let the West put forward its point of view as forcefully as it can, but let it respect their neutrality.

Mr. Nehru tells us that 'the dependant countries of Asia and Africa are thirsting for freedom and economic progress'. It is strange indeed, he pointed out, that it should be the communists who appear as liberators in these areas. There is no baulking the fact. Mr. Nehru's words depict with accuracy the situation in Asia. The pendulum must be swung in favour of the West and that can only be achieved by appearing as true liberators, mindful of all local susceptibilities, motivated by a deep respect for all the peoples of Asia and Africa.

The corollary of this respect for neutrality is equality of treatment accorded to all nations. The Russian leaders have shown how attuned their propaganda is to this great need of all the uncommitted countries.

In their relations with other countries the Western world must adopt a policy which no longer assumes that the West knows best. Such an attitude, even when justified, is offensive, creates suspicion, and fails to inspire genuine friendship. In the same way in which a candidate to office in a democratic country, however exalted a personage he may be, needs even the humblest votes;

in the same way in which a candidate, however eminent, is prepared to prove his worth and convince his often ignorant electorate that power should be entrusted into his hands, so the West must today convince the uncommitted nations that it and not the communists is at the head of those progressive forces which hold out a promise of better things to come for the under-privileged everywhere in the world.

VIII

PRESENT CONTRADICTIONS

WHAT is Western policy today? One may well ask, and many do ask constantly, with a sinking heart. An Egyptian would wonder whether the West will let him work towards the ideal of Arab unity, but will probably decide that the West wishes to divide the whole Middle East area in order better to control it. An Israeli would ask whether the West is prepared to help him establish firmly his new-found home, but will probably conclude that it is in the West's interest to make friends with the Arabs and ignore little Israel. A Cypriot yearns for his independence. He is told he cannot have it because Cyprus is strategically important in the face of the communist danger and must be kept under direct Western control. An Indian wants to be left alone to build up his vast country and to cope with the terrible problems of poverty and over-population. He sees himself constantly urged to join this or that Western system of military alliance, which he interprets as a direct threat to his freedom of action within his own country. An Algerian wants a measure of agreement with the French which will give him the right to be master in his own house, but Algeria is part of Metropolitan France and seemingly all important to the very existence of N.A.T.O.

No one concerned with politics in any capacity expects perfection. No one pretends that all difficult problems can be resolved overnight. But the world wants a clear lead. The Western Powers can, and must, give it.

Instead of a negative approach, moving haphazardly from one

crisis to another, in an effort to counter the communist moves as they are made, the West must produce a positive approach which will capture the imagination of mankind before it is too late. Once such a clear lead is given, then the Western powers must try to achieve consistency, to solve all immediate problems to the best of their ability and in keeping with the spirit of the lead they have given.

A few examples will illustrate the point. The Summit meeting at Geneva was only possible because the Western countries did not dare to jettison the notion of a world united in peace and striving to keep peace. In the congenial atmosphere of Geneva Sir Anthony Eden invited Krushchev and Bulganin to pay a state visit to Great Britain. The invitation was accepted, but soon after the Soviet leaders abused Britain in offensive language during their tour of South-East Asia. At the 20th Soviet Communist Party Congress a gradual but inevitable destruction of all capitalist governments was confidently restated as an aim. Nevertheless the invitation was not cancelled and the Russian leaders duly arrived in Great Britain in April 1956 for a ten-day state visit, bringing with them gifts and tempting trade offers to the tune of £800 to £1,000 millions. No tangible results were achieved apart from the temporary lifting of Soviet jamming of B.B.C. broadcasts in Russian. But Britain's well-wishers in the uncommitted world watched the puzzling spectacle of Britain's detractors being received by the Queen with unconcealed anxiety. 'What was the purpose of the visit?' they asked. The fact that they were invited at all as honoured guests could only strain relations with Britain's allies across the Atlantic and create confusion and despondency among the uncommitted nations and the peoples now under the communist yoke. But the British government was saved from appearing hasty in having initiated the visit in the first place by the sober, cool, yet polite reception which the British people extended to the Soviet leaders.

The Americans have organised a most efficient instrument of psychological warfare in the shape of the 'Free Europe' Organisation. With its headquarters in New York, this organisation beams regular radio programmes to the countries of Eastern Europe, in certain cases with round-the-clock programmes and in direct competition with the communist-controlled national broadcasting stations. Officially, the United States disclaims any knowledge of, or connection with the Free Europe Organisation. This can only lead to misrepresentation or charges of perfidy. The communist leaders avoid the same mistake. They shout it from the roof-tops that they want to liberate all nations from their capitalist exploiters who now control their governments. They have dealings with those governments until the time is ripe for liberation by revolution, or, particularly since the 20th Congress of the Russian Communist Party, by democratic process. If 'Free Europe' is truly a private American organisation entirely financed from private funds and therefore all the more valuable and perfectly in keeping with America's traditions of free initiative, then the charges of perfidy can easily be avoided by the open declaration of the American Government of its approval of this psychological warfare, which is after all only a more efficient war on the air than the war waged against the West by the communist-controlled radio stations.

Berlin is an advanced post of democracy, the only remaining democratic enclave within the communist world. The West defended its position there in a spectacular fashion at the time of the highly successful air-lift which broke the Russian blockade. But democracy in West Berlin would be doomed were it not for the courage and determination of the Berlin people themselves. Nevertheless, at a conference in Berlin on November 19th, 1955, the West was charged with lack of foresight and the failure to explore Soviet intentions before going to Geneva. The slogan of the conference was: 'Berlin appeals to the world—We shall not resign ourselves to Geneva.' If a positive, long-term Western world policy is found, such charges would no longer be justified.

Germany is one of the most strategically important countries, for political as well as military reasons. But Dr. Adenauer's position in Germany has been greatly weakened by the Western failure to have a clear-sighted long-term policy *vis-à-vis* the Soviet Union. In the wake of the Geneva Summit meeting Adenauer went to Moscow, and re-established diplomatic relations, although the Soviet Government fully supports the East German Republic. It is quite correct that Adenauer obtained in exchange the release of some 10,000 German prisoners of war still held in Russia. But the price he had to pay was heavy and the West German position with regard to the East German People's Republic undermined. The Western Powers could not obtain the release of the German prisoners, but Germany succeeded by negotiating direct with Moscow. No wonder more and more people in West Germany argue today that, since the West cannot obtain Germany's re-unification, Germany might do so by direct negotiations with the Kremlin and, if need be, with the Eastern German Republic as well. The demand for such direct approach is growing. The German Free Democratic Party have now broken the coalition, gone into opposition and joined the swelling ranks of those who want Germany to secure unification, even if this means taking again the long road to Moscow. This situation could have been avoided. The false hopes of Geneva and the hope and confidence placed in the effectiveness of Western negotiation with Russia, on the question of Germany unity, should never have been allowed to become so great for they had no justification in fact. Thus the correspondingly great disappointment in West Germany, and the loss of face for the West, would have been avoided.

One final example. The discussions on disarmament soon ran

into difficulties at the Foreign Ministers' Conference in November 1955. The Western Powers put forward three proposals, the Eisenhower plan for aerial inspection, the Eden plan for inspection of forces in a limited area to be defined on either side of the Iron Curtain, and the Faure plan for a reduction of both armed forces and arms production by means of a stringent budgetary control. The Russians proposed the adoption of an immediate ban on the use of all atomic weapons and the Bulganin plan for ground inspection of forces by means of setting up control posts at strategic points. The Soviet Minister rejected the Western proposals on spurious grounds and the Western representatives could not accept the banning of atomic weapons before their own proposals were accepted which, they claimed, alone provided sufficient guarantee that the use of atomic weapons would be effectively abandoned. To break the deadlock the Western Ministers, particularly Mr. Dulles, tried to find a compromise solution. A new proposal was submitted which was to include the salient points of all the plans proposed. Nevertheless, Molotov refused to accept the new proposals.

The Western Foreign Ministers were absolutely right to try to find a solution by compromise, hard bargaining and negotiation. No one can deny that any measures which effectively reduce armaments and the number of forces under arms are beneficial to world peace and reduce international tension, provided, of course, that the security of the free world should not thereby be impaired. However, after the conference was concluded without any agreement being reached at all, the wisdom of Mr. Dulles's comments was open to question. He said, among other things, that the Eisenhower-Bulganin system 'constitutes a decisive initial step in providing against the possibility of a great surprise attack'. He showed optimism as to the possibility of making further advances towards a final and complete agreement. It is perfectly understandable that an official communiqué should contain an element of optimism. But Mr. Dulles's direct reference to the 'Eisenhower-Bulganin system' was unfortunate.

Negotiations between East and West are necessary, and the reduction of international tension must continue to be a positive aim. Any point on which a compromise solution that safeguards some interest of the West is possible should always be sought and accepted. But in accepting a compromise solution the democratic West must clearly show that it is an imperfect solution, falling far short of Western ideals and Western objectives. Any system that may arise from such a compromise should under no circumstances bear the name of one of the most prominent Western leaders. The psychological effect of a statement like that of Mr. Dulles, on the subject peoples of Russia, and even on the uncommitted nations of the world, cannot be anything but disastrous. They will link up President Eisenhower's name with that of Bulganin, their oppressor, and blame them together for creating and maintaining a system which perpetuates their slavery.

IX

THE ESSENCE OF THE CONFLICT

'IF it is to be a battle of ideas, fairly waged, then we have nothing to fear and fear nothing,' said Selwyn Lloyd in the House of Commons in February 1956. Those are fine words. They correctly express the profound conflict which torments humanity in the mid-twentieth century.

The nature of the conflict strikes at the very roots of life, for the present challenge is fundamental. As our knowledge of it improves the forces ranged on either side of the barricade acquire more substance and reality. On one side there are those who believe that there is an intrinsic worth in human existence, that life, mysteriously given, has to be lived out by every single member of the community; that the seed of life, planted in us for a purpose which we often fail to understand, transcends our power of control; that all our endeavours can only aim at promoting those conditions which give life fuller scope and better chances of self-expression. On the other side are those who regard life as a mere accident of evolution. Human existence is the pinnacle, the climax of a million years of gradual development on earth; and also perhaps only a stage towards an even higher existence. For them life has no intrinsic worth, and is justified only in so far as it is a contributory factor to that of further human development.

On the one side are the forces which derive their inspiration from a religious approach to life, their ranks joined by atheistic humanists. Thousands of years of struggle have produced the noble ideas of the West and created the institutions which aim constantly to improve the conditions in which each individual life can find its expression and is given free play in the great design of existence. These institutions have come to be known as democracy.

Opposed to these institutions are those who derive their inspiration exclusively from science. They have grown more articulate since the industrial revolution and have steadily gained strength, particularly after the discovery of the scientific 'laws', which govern society and all social phenomena. When he knew he was doomed, during the last days of the Saló Republic, Mussolini told his fanatical young disciples, Mezzasoma and Pavolini: 'Fascism is a product of the modern crisis, the crisis of Man, who can no longer remain within the normal bounds of life with its conventionalism, within the bounds of the existing human laws. I would call it irrationalism. There is such a thing as morality but we are tired of it. I'd go further and say that it makes no impression on us. That can be changed by going against the stream. We are tormented people. Every one of us would like to be the sun, the pole of life, for himself and for others. There you have the evil at the heart of modern Man, call it irrationalism, Bolshevism, Fascism.' With the clear-sightedness of the man who no longer expects anything from life, but who has struggled throughout a lifetime for mastery, Mussolini accepted defeat and saw in his last days that he had been struggling against the morality which Western civilisation has brought into being and which rests on the belief that each human existence has an intrinsic value. He ranged his attempt to reject that basic morality on the side of those who make a God out of man and on the side of the far more powerful and coherent bid to dethrone Western morality in the name of science, which is Bolshevism.

Since the successful communist revolution of about forty years ago, the communist bid for world dominion has been gathering momentum and has advanced from victory to victory during the last decade because its real nature has not been fully realised, or if realised not acted upon by those who are the trustees of the peoples of Western civilisation. Mr. Dulles had the temerity to declare before a Congressional committee in March 1956 that 'the Communist policies have gradually ceased to produce results. They (the communists) have got to re-vamp their whole creed from A—Z . . . The unity and firmness and resolution of the free nations during the past few years have caused the Soviet policy to fail and today they are trying to figure out how they are going to get a better one.' This appraisal of the situation shows a profound lack of understanding and denies the glaring reality of the terrifying successes which the communists have piled up in the last few years. It ignores the fact that today communism appears to be the upholder of their just aspirations to countless millions outside the communist world.

This is ideological war; all the more difficult because it is a war of attrition. If the West is to prevail in the battle of ideas, it must have the courage of its convictions and prove that it stands for clear objectives. Its sincerity will be proved in time if the logical consequences of its aims are willingly accepted and acted upon by the Western leaders, particularly if this process is achieved by surrendering some immediate advantage. The sincerity of the West will be proved if reality is accepted squarely and the battle of ideas entered upon openly. By giving up the concept of one-world-united-in-peace-and-for-peace the West openly declares itself opposed to tyranny everywhere. By denouncing slave labour and the mass murder of millions of people carried out in Soviet Russia and, more recently, in Mao's China, and by protesting against the mass deportation of young Hungarians, whose only guilt was their readiness to fight for freedom, the West proclaims its unequivocal belief in the rights of Man. By renouncing imperialism and colonialism, by the material proof of its profound belief in the equality of all nations, by respecting neutrality and removing the taint of racialism from all its policies, the West will be able to enrol the powerful force of nationalism, a force which can be made to work for the good of mankind. This is no mean task. It requires a revision of the paraphernalia of present-day Western policy. But if it is carried out with courage, determination and consistency, the sincerity of the West will be proved.

Parallel with this inevitably painful operation the West can and must embark upon a constructive policy of co-ordinating those forces upon which Western democracy can rely with absolute certainty. The removal of the deadwood of Western policy, the legacy of the past, will make it possible for the West to devise and apply a new positive policy which will prove not only its sincerity but also its readiness and ability to make the great victories of democracy for Western Man available throughout the world. New declarations of purposes should be made. They will be regarded with respect and the cause of Man against tyranny will steadily advance, *pari passu*, with the measures which the West will then take, to turn those declarations into reality.

X

A POSITIVE POLICY

IT is not the purpose of this book to set out in detail the exact course of action which the Western Powers ought to take in order to rise to the challenge of the hour. Such an attempt would merely lay it wide open to charges of Utopianism and advancement of pet schemes. Besides, the working out of the chosen instruments of action properly belongs to highly skilled national and international civil services. They alone, stimulated and guided by Western statesmen, are in possession of all the relevant data to merge the desirable with the possible, to find workable solutions, and to lay the foundations of viable institutions. Given the high degree of efficiency, selflessness and industry, which these bodies customarily place at the service of the state, there is no need to doubt that, once the right approach has been adopted, their proposed solutions will serve the good of all those who believe in democracy and are ready to make sacrifices to defend, and further advance throughout the world, those democratic liberties which are so much in peril today. Nevertheless, it may be permissible to indicate the broad outlines and the principal desiderata of Western policy today: not as a dogmatic statement of what is required, but as a set of ideas for discussion, for adoption, rejection or modification. What is important is not so much to have this or that suggestion adopted but to get the policy-makers to think about fundamentals.

The problem is clear. The West has a defensive policy; its whole structure is fundamentally based on fear. How to stop communism? This is the question which seems to be the permanent preoccupation of Western statesmen. The West must find a positive policy with such a powerful appeal throughout the world that it would force the communists into the position of looking for means to prevent the further spread of democracy. If this were achieved the West would have embarked upon a constructive approach with the whole world as its field. Thus the communist problem would be reduced to its proper size; it would become only one, if still the most important, of the many problems the West has to solve in the interests of humanity.

Western democracy is in duty bound before history to grasp the opportunity and to accept the responsibility of championing the free institutions which it treasures. But if the West fails to sense the tragic urgency of the unforgiving hour and continues on its present suicidal policy, tomorrow it may be too late.

The principles which must guide Western action can be stated very briefly. They are not many.

First the West must unite under one banner all the reliable forces which desire to uphold the free institutions of democracy. It must unite all truly democratic states, all true democrats wherever they may be.

Secondly, the West must make it clear that the benefits of democracy can be made available to all nations, for the individual benefit of all people.

Finally, the West must pledge itself to work for the spreading abroad of the benefits which only democracy can confer, even at the cost of accepting temporary sacrifices.

XI

UNITY

THE approach to the actual steps which must be taken to produce the positive policy here advocated, must necessarily be tentative and exploratory. The broad outlines, however, are clear.

In the first place, the West must unite all democratic states by persuasion, not by force. Democracy must make its purpose obvious in the United Nations Organisation. No matter how few they may be at the beginning, the democratic states will stand together and present a solid, united front. They must constantly demand, at all their international conferences and negotiations, that the communist powers should (*a*) desist from further aggression and (*b*) release all nations which they now keep in subjection against their will.

Such an attitude will be understood throughout the world, even if results are a long time in coming. Negotiations with the communist powers should only be conducted on a strict bargaining basis. Whatever settlements are agreed it must be made crystal clear that they are a temporary means of finding a *modus vivendi* in an imperfect world, without in any way prejudicing the persistently reiterated demand of the West that the communist powers abandon aggression and release their subject peoples.

Dr. Adenauer's suggestion that N.A.T.O.—a defence organisation which binds together like-minded democratic nations—should be expanded into a political instrument of the free world, is very interesting. It may be well worth further exploration.

What is undoubtedly important is that all functioning democracies, wherever they may be, Australia, New Zealand, Uruguay, etc., should be brought together in one over-all democratic organisation.

In this connection Mr. Nehru's appraisal of the value of the Commonwealth is highly significant. He staunchly defends its merits. He declared that membership of the Commonwealth, far from restricting India's scope of action, gave her greater freedom. And he expressed his hope that the Commonwealth might gradually develop into world citizenship.

The idea of an expanding commonwealth of independent nations, linked together by their common bond of adherence to parliamentary democracy, is now put forward with more and more insistence by imaginative thinkers from the back benches of the present House of Commons.

At the Council of Europe the idea of co-ordinated European policy for Africa was boldly considered as welcome and valuable by France, now in the toils of finding a solution for her North African problems. The movement towards a United States of Europe and M. Monnet's 'Action Committee', as well as the Messina agreement and the various integrating proposals through the O.E.E.C., are all movements in the right direction. Greater integration of the democratic states, linked together in independence, must be constantly aimed at so that they should together defend and champion the ideals which they serve and practise. Old schemes and new, so long as they improve relations within the community of democratic countries, are beneficial. They must be judged and encouraged on their own merits, whether they produce greater unity, even if they may only encompass a few countries or only part of the area where democracy exists. But the important thing is to devise an over-all organisation which will be the centre of attraction for all states who take a definite stand against communism. Coal and steel may be

165

regulated in Western Europe by one organisation, atomic energy by another, tariffs and trade by yet a third, all partly overlapping, even if not exactly covering the same membership. But the vital desideratum today is to have a central organ which operates a *long-term* democratic policy scrupulously applied by all democratic states *vis-à-vis* the communist world.

Such an organisation would be a powerful centripetal force, attracting by its self-imposed discipline all nations who value the democratic way of life.

Three arguments and criticisms immediately spring to mind.

First: who is to define which nations qualify for this community of democratic nations? The answer is straightforward—the democratic nations united in council, themselves. There need be no searching of hearts on this problem, there need be no misgiving or hesitation. It is easy enough to determine whether or not a country guarantees a minimum of rights to the individual. A credentials committee could easily be devised, born of and serving the purposes of the democratic community. A parallel will illustrate the point. The Communist Party of Great Britain has repeatedly applied for membership of the Labour Party. The application has always been rejected, not by an outside body but by the Labour Party Conference itself, year after year. Yet no one can accuse the Labour Party of not abiding by democratic principles.

In the second place, it may be argued that the very purpose of democracy is diversity, that by creating such an organisation the very essence of democracy is sacrificed. This is an utterly fallacious argument already exposed and rejected. The principles and values of democracy, far from suffering as a result of unity, are enhanced whenever self-discipline for the sake of unity is practised. Participation in N.A.T.O., far from denying internal democracy in any of the member countries, brings a greater enjoyment to all from the sense of security which is derived from it.

Finally it has often been argued that coalitions are necessarily ineffectual. It is extraordinary that this *canard* should still carry weight when the greatest victories against tyranny, from the days of the city-states of ancient Greece to those of modern times, were won by coalitions. In the initial stages of a conflict tyranny always has powerful advantages which often hold the promise of victory. But coalitions, precisely because they are freely entered upon by choice, are capable of mustering far greater spiritual and moral strength than the monolithic structure of tyranny; always provided, of course, that coalition is not the result of dragooning, bribery, and immediate selfish advantage.

It is useless, however, to attempt to present a united front when there is none. It is not numbers that count.

XII

RALLYING OF DEMOCRATIC FORCES

THE Western Powers deal at government level with governments in power. A consequence of this is the reluctance of Western governments to recognise a newly established revolutionary régime. The exercise of caution in giving such recognition is admirable, and justified. But the fountain-spring of this reluctance, which is the principle of dealing only with established governments, is out of date. The battle of ideas today must be entered into at all levels. Western policy must be addressed to the peoples of the world in the name of the defence of the rights of the individual. The communist policy is perfectly attuned for world conquest precisely because it deals at government level with governments, the legality of which they reject, but addresses the whole weight of their policy of 'liberation' to the people of the whole world. This effective approach applied by communist policy must be matched by a policy which presents a challenge to each human being wherever he may be in the world, if he believes that his rights as a man are worth fighting for. Each human being who considers himself a democrat, a lover of individual freedom and liberty, must know where his salvation can come from. Only by creating a visible centre which can fulfil his aspirations and from which he can derive support in his own struggle for democracy wherever he may be, will the individual fighter for freedom find the strength which he so sorely needs today.

The West must today rally all democrats and give them consciously and openly, not only the much-needed sense of belonging, but also the sense of direction which is essential to any successful endeavour.

It is strange how the lessons of history have been forgotten. It is strange how today the millions of refugees from tyranny are considered 'displaced persons', awkward individuals who create problems in the West by not readily integrating themselves in the general fabric of Western society. It is strange how often they are regarded as pariahs, flotsam and jetsam aimlessly thrown about by the political waves of the world. Their usefulness to Western society not being immediately apparent, they are conveniently dubbed big landlords, remnants of feudal systems and, generally, reactionary elements who naturally mourn for their lost privileges. They inspire pity in the best of cases, but their struggle is hardly understood. Their countries are far away, and the rumble of war and forced 'revolution', which deprived them of their national independence, is too distant in time and space to bridge the unforgiving silence in between. Yet the annals of history bear incontrovertible witness that invasion after invasion from the East has been slowed down on the European Eastern marches by the will and sacrifice of the people who live there, thus giving the West a warning and a respite to repel the danger which threatened its very existence. So it is in our own age. First Poland and Rumania, in 1945, then one by one the other East European States, until finally the West became aware of the imminent danger when Czechoslovakia fell under the communists in 1948. These people are European, and proud of being European in every sense of the word. They cherish the ideals of the West and, if at times their institutions were not as perfect as those of the West, there was good cause for their slow progress, since it was always interrupted by wars and armed conflicts. They desire, with their every fibre, freedom for the individual, and they aspire to the democratic institutions which the West has created.

Though it may not realise it, the West greatly benefited from their sacrifice and sorely needs their help in the present struggle. So long as the love of freedom is not extinct in Eastern Europe the communist bid for world power will bear the seeds of disintegration and destruction in its body politic. The greatest quality of the Eastern European peoples is resilience. Hundreds of years of foreign domination have failed to curb their spirit. Today, the tyranny of the invader is harsher and greater than ever before, but their thirst for freedom is unquenched.

It is stranger still that the West forgets its own history. It forgets, for instance, the lessons of the nineteenth century. When reaction finally triumphed in Europe, a century ago, and the great principles of 1848 were abandoned in the name of stability, the West, and particularly Britain, not only welcomed the great Central and East European democratic leaders of those days, but offered them ready platforms from which to expound their views in the service of the ideal of liberty. It is forgotten that Palmerston championed the rights of distant people, the enslaved Bulgarians, and actually fought a general election, embodying the plight of the Bulgarians in his political platform. There were others like him before and after him.

If Western democracy chooses to give only perfunctory support to the struggle of the East European people, and all but ignores the contribution which the exiles can make to the common cause, the communist governments, installed in Eastern Europe by Soviet arms, make no such mistake—a complete proof, if such were still needed, that the continued fight for liberty of the exiles is highly important. Indeed, it is clear that their determined opposition to communist tyranny finds powerful response in the hearts of the people in their own countries. This the communist governments fully realise. They are aware that so long as an important *émigré* movement remains alive they cannot hope to consolidate their power. Consequently they seek to destroy it. A highly efficient organisation was set up at Pankow in East

Berlin for the specific purpose of producing a movement in reverse—of bringing about the voluntary repatriation of all politically conscious exiles. The action of this Pankow organisation is powerfully supported by every communist government. A specially instituted radio station broadcasts direct appeals for repatriation from the families of the *émigrés*, and the spokesmen of this organisation constantly describe the wonderful life enjoyed in the home country in its mighty constructive effort, and the plight of the refugees who are cold-shouldered in the free world. They publish excellent newspapers, posted in carefully sealed envelopes, to every exile whose address they manage to find. They send their agents to establish personal contact with all those who show the slightest wavering or inclination to return. Special decrees of amnesty for political offences have been adopted in every satellite country, and personal freedom and a job are repeatedly 'guaranteed' to every returned exile. They have achieved notable, though limited, success, but the returned exiles add their voice to that of the 'reformed' democratic leaders who, after a period of imprisonment, consented to come before the microphones and appeal to the exiles to return home. This intense activity is fully supported at government level.

The Soviet delegate at the Social, Humanitarian and Cultural Committee in October 1955, for example, boldly asked the Assembly to demand that the United Nations assist in the return to the East of about 300,000 refugees by using its influence with the countries of asylum, with a view to stopping propaganda and permitting Eastern representatives to persuade the exiles to return.

XIII

'PEACE, FREEDOM, PROSPERITY'

IN the present struggle against communism the democratic West needs all the support which it can get. Not only in the Western countries, not only in the areas now held by the communists, but also in the rest of the world. By creating a World Council of Democracy which would include all countries who freely unite for the purpose of upholding the ideals of the West, a directing organ would come into being. In order to give an outward expression to the interest which the West takes in the fate of democracy everywhere, a periodic World Congress of Democracy could be held. At this congress all democratic parties, now functioning in the free world, could be invited, as well as representatives and observers from countries which at present do not enjoy democratic freedoms. This congress could well work on the main problems which affect the world today. It could have its working committees, inviting suggestions from all representatives, framing resolutions which would then be adopted by the Congress as recommendations to be passed for action to the World Council of Democracy.

The advantages to be derived from action along such lines are easily discernible. The World Council of Democracy could have its planning board, and its policy evaluation department. It could set up an information organisation which, with the powerful means of mass communication now available, could keep the whole world fully informed, not only of its policies and intentions, but also of its solid achievements for the common people everywhere. The almost morbid preoccupation with the military aspect of the communist challenge, with problems of security, alliances, and various other 'physical' measures for stemming the communist tide, would give way to considerations of what could be done on a world-wide scale to improve the lot of the under-privileged nations.

At one stroke the tables would be turned. The present vacilla-tion and disjointed action, independently pursued by the various democratic states, and all too often contradictory, would give place to a unity of command. No action in the battle of ideas would be undertaken without first being considered and ap-proved. No move would be made without first appraising its long-term as well as its immediate consequences.

Monsieur Pineau, like Dr. Adenauer before him, raised pre-cisely this point at the luncheon given for him by the Anglo-American Press Association in Paris, immediately after he announced the French Government's acceptance of the invitation to go to Moscow in May 1956. Other statesmen and soldiers whose patriotism cannot be questioned advocate the same course.

Unity of command means purposefulness, flexibility and long-term planning. It grasps the initiative and holds it firmly ever after. A permanent secretariat, together with its various agencies, could carry out with the resources at its disposal the resolutions passed by the World Congress of Democracy. The secretariat could serve as the centralised organ, keeping a watchful eye on world developments with special reference to democracy's progress from country to country. It would receive appeals, resolutions and complaints from every corner of the world. Reports, like the banning of public meetings in Bangkok by Field-Marshal Pibul Songgram, or the findings of the Inter-national Press Institute showing that pressure against the freedom of the press is increasing, could be tabulated, evaluated, and appropriate action suggested to the governments most interested in the matter. If necessary they would be brought before the annual congress for further discussion.

One of the most important advantages, resulting from the establishment of a permanent secretariat, besides those of a strictly political nature, would be found in the possibility of increasing the area of contact between East and West in all fields, without any detriment to the West.

The three main problems in the world today, as always, are peace, freedom, and prosperity.

The Congress could suggest solutions for peace, for the problems of *security*. If peace is threatened in any particular area, through communist intervention or subversion, the Congress could recommend solutions which would inevitably mean co-operation between various countries in the threatened area with the backing and full support of the major democratic states. But the difference between having such an action suggested to the Western Powers, through some international body like a World Congress of Democracy, by the threatened people themselves, with the concurrence of all other represented nations, and action through Western-created military defensive systems, is a difference of substance. If action were to be taken as a result of a recommendation made by the World Congress of Democracy, then under no circumstances could the West be accused of imperialism as it is frequently accused today, both in the Middle East and in South-East Asia. If the problems of peace are thus treated, year after year, or every two or three years, by a World Congress of Democracy, all nations represented would acquire the feeling of a newly won equality.

Today, it is the United States and the democratic West who must take the first steps in organising the armed forces and the weapons necessary to prevent aggression and maintain peace. It is primarily the United States, Britain and France who must take the unpopular military measures in order to maintain peace. All the major Western democracies are profoundly peaceful; but, because of the international situation today created by potential communist aggression, they must prepare themselves for war, and talk war to other countries in order to maintain peace. This unenviable situation has led, to a large extent, to the partial success of communist propaganda among the uncommitted nations which now consider the communists as a party of peace, and think the West, and particularly America, if not war-minded, war-obsessed, and not infrequently accept the communist charges that important pressure groups in America actively work to start a world war. The fact that a democracy never wants to start a war, either of aggression or of 'prevention', makes too small an impact on the uncommitted nations of the world. As long as the relationship of the West to the uncommitted nations is mainly centred around the problem of security and deals predominantly with military commitments, bases, alliances and the sinews of war generally, it is inevitable that the charge of war-mongering and war-mindedness should stick. The communists offer economic agreements, on a relatively modest scale, but without strings, and propose friendship. It is completely immaterial that these treaties are always political in design and always used to further the fortunes of communism. If the representatives of all the democratic countries in the world, joined by the democrats coming from countries where democracy either does not exist or is submerged by tyranny, were to thrash out the problem of security in the appropriate committee of a World Congress of Democracy, then any intervention by the Western Powers, any military step which they were required to make, would be a peaceful action in the service of peace. All Western action would be the result of joint decision, undertaken at the request of the threatened nation.

Such an organisation could nail down effectively all communist lies. It would prove to all doubters that the West only intervenes at the request and for the benefit of the people of the area which is threatened.

The importance for the West of doing something on these lines is so great that it cannot be overstated. The charge of new imperialism would be proved utterly baseless if the presence of Americans in any country were the result of an invitation from the country concerned and at the recommendation put forward by a working committee at a World Congress of Democracy.

Besides security, a second essential set of problems, which could be served with great effectiveness through such a world organisation, are those connected with *freedom*. A working committee on freedom at the World Congress of Democracy could estimate the progress, or retrogression of freedom year by year in all countries of the world. The main task of this committee on freedom could be the examination of claims for independence; the putting forward of recommendations as to which of these claims ought to go one step further and be presented to the Council of Democracy, whose permanent secretariat could then take it up with the countries who jointly adhered to the declaration for the winding up of colonialism. The whole development of colonialism could be encouraged to evolve along such clear, constitutional lines. A gradual advance could be offered, and the machinery provided, so that the impartiality of the decision would be unquestionable.

Today, nothing the West will do, no concession that the West will make, will remove completely the charge of colonialism. The Pakistanis, for instance, owe their national existence, against the claims of their fellow countrymen, solely to the support and justice which they received at the hands of Britain. Pakistan retained her link with the British Crown when India turned republic. Later, she entered into the two defensive systems created by the West in South-East Asia and the Middle East. She received important material support from the West. Yet the Constituent Assembly of Pakistan elected to break the ties with the British Crown and declared Pakistan an Islamic Republic within the Commonwealth. The impetus of the rising nationalism in the uncommitted nations is tremendous. So far, the West has chosen to recognise it only grudgingly. The West must not only recognise it, but encourage it, and make it its friend. The present policy of concessions and, as in the case of the Caribbean or Malaya, even of encouraging and speeding-up voluntarily the process of self-determination, though very enlightened, is wholly insufficient to cope with the situation. As long as one single speck of land remains under the rule of the Western Powers the communist charge of colonialism will stick. Short of immediately winding up all the colonial possessions of all the Western Powers, which could only mean chaos, the communists will be able to appear to the world as the friend of the colonial people because they never cease to press for the winding up of all colonialism. The situation, however, can be reversed completely, by providing the necessary 'constitutional' machinery for advancement towards independence, by making it available to all, and sanctifying it in international law.

But the Western Powers must never be put on the defensive, never be forced to deny, by their own action, a demand for a further advance towards independence once such a demand is made. Such demands should be made, or referred to a World Congress of Democracy, and examined by its working committee on Freedom. It should be for this committee to decide whether the demand is justified or not. In other words, already at this initial stage, the rejection of the demand can be made by an independent body which cannot be charged under any circumstances with partiality for the Western Powers. If the demand is justified the working committee would make recommendation to the Council of Democracy and entrust its permanent secretariat to take up the matter with the colonial power concerned, or, better still, with a Council of all colonial powers, signatories of the joint declaration for the winding up of colonialism. Only then should action be taken.

The advantages of such a procedure are obvious. The pursuit of independence and freedom, through violence, would immediately prejudice the case for the claimant. If a parallel is wanted one could compare the situation with an illegal strike. By refusing to use the existing machinery for settling an industrial dispute the strikers go against their own organisation, the trade union and against legality. The feeling of the country will inevitably be against them. From the beginning the claimants for further advance towards independence who resort to violence put themselves in the wrong.

Another advantage offered by such a procedure is the time lag between the moment the claim is registered and the moment action has to be taken. This period would give both parties the opportunity to sort out essentials from incidentals, allow tempers to cool, and permit a sensible solution of the problem to be found.

Finally, the greatest advantage of all is that no charge of colonialism could ever again be attached to the Western Powers. The communist bid for world conquest would be deprived of one of the most powerful weapons which it uses so effectively today.

A third set of problems which would come within the compass of a World Congress of Democracy are those connected with the problem of *prosperity*. Today, the Western Powers, but particularly the Americans, are spending vast sums in helping underdeveloped countries on the road to prosperity. This enormous wealth, devoted to the help of others, is not achieving the desired results. A staggering sum has already been spent by the Western Powers on the Eastern nations in technical assistance and in direct financial aid, as well as in aid through the various agencies of the United Nations.[1] The United States alone has earmarked for the 1956–7 fiscal year $1,420,000,000 as *non-military* aid to Asia, the Middle East and South America. This is a tremendous increase if it is compared with the $565 million spent in 1952. India alone received between March 1951 and January 1956, that is, during the period of her first five-year plan, approximately £230 million. On top of this there has been American aid in the form of a wheat loan of $190 million. Egypt is also

[1] The following tables, published in the *Manchester Guardian*, 25th January 1956, give an idea of the magnitude of present Western effort for Eastern nations alone:

American technical assistance programmes for the fiscal year, 1st July 1955 to 30th June 1956:

	million		million
Afghanistan	$2	Philippines	$5·9
Nepal	$1	Egypt	$4
Pakistan	$6	Iraq	$2·3
India	$10	Israel	$1·5
Indonesia	$11·1	Lebanon	$2
		Jordan	$2·6

By April 1956 Great Britain had already spent some £1·9 million and has agreed to make available some £7 million over the next six years.

Direct American non-military aid during the 1955 fiscal year:

	million		million
Iran	$86	Korea	$207
Israel	$30	Nepal	$1
Jordan	$13	India	$50
Libya	$10	Egypt	$8

Under the Colombo Plan the Export-Import Bank has authorised development credits for the last five years amounting to about $127 million to Indonesia, Thailand and the Philippines.

Finally, some $30 million were contributed by Britain and the United States to the specialised agencies of the United Nations.

receiving great sums of money. In the Middle East as a whole, the current American figure of *non-military* aid is $28.4 million, etc. etc.

One could point out the enormous economic, *non-military* support which the West has given the uncommitted nations. Yet this material sacrifice, which, in effect, the West is making, has achieved next to nothing. On the contrary, all trained and objective observers constantly report that the West is losing ground, and the friendship of the uncommitted nations. The *Manchester Guardian* (22nd December 1955) rightly said: 'The general experience has been that the way to incur popular odium is to offer economic aid.'

The Soviet Powers, who have given incomparably smaller economic assistance to the uncommitted nations,[1] have achieved a considerable success in this field. They wish to appear, and are largely accepted by the uncommitted nations, as brothers, ready to 'share their last piece of bread' for the advancement of all under-developed countries, but especially those of South-East Asia.

This problem, in all its gravity, is already appreciated by Western statesmen. It is clear that the present policy is not achieving its aims and that there is nothing except resentment and antagonism to show in exchange for the aid given.

M. Pineau, the French Foreign Minister, has spoken of a 'dynamic, aggressive, economic policy', which in his opinion is now needed, but did not define it. Dr. Erhard, the German Minister of Economics, has spoken of the creation by the Messina Powers (France, Britain, Italy, and the Benelux countries) of a common market and then entering into important trade relations with the under-developed countries of the uncommitted world. He pointed to the lurking danger of communist competition.

[1] Total communist aid promises: $500 millions; actual communist aid (delivered): $23.4 millions; actual U.S.A. aid (delivered): $37,000 millions.

Through dumping of heavily subsidised exports, the Soviet system, with its centralised control, is able to capture or disrupt foreign markets in a way with which no single firm and no single European country can successfully compete. M. Pineau further suggested that the solution must lie in the concerted action of the Messina Powers, or better still in the concerted action of all Western Powers, in face of the deliberate communist policy of capturing certain markets for political purposes.

James D. Zellerbach, the Chairman of the United States Committee for Economic Development, has spoken of the 'need to create inducements for United States firms, by such means as lower corporate taxes on overseas earnings, to devote more of their resources to trading and investing in the under-developed countries'. And he also underlined the fundamental need, that the West should help the under-developed countries to 'build up their countries instead of going in only to offset the Russians'.

The disastrous results of the economic policy now pursed are recognised by all responsible people who are ready to face the facts. The Russians themselves are supremely confident that they can completely destroy the reputation of the West and annihilate Western economic action in the uncommitted world. They are supremely confident that Western disunity, individual greed and the 'basic contradictions' of capitalism, will prevent the formulation of an effective Western economic policy. Khrushchev said in Moscow in November 1955: 'Your system will collapse through economic competition with the socialist camp, not through the help of the Soviet Union. It is a natural historical development.'

What is the cause of the failure of Western economic policy?

In the first place it is because of the stigma attached to all economic aid as being 'with strings'. Mr. Nehru rightly said: 'The ways and means of giving aid are far more important even than the amounts.' He implied that in certain quarters the idea predominates that one could buy a country and that 'aid should be given only after tearing to shreds the self-respect of the recipient by depicting it either on the brink of bankruptcy, or on the verge of political suicide. In fact, by pretending that it has got to be saved against its better judgment'. (*Manchester Guardian*, 29th February 1956.)

The policy of making aid available only in order to prevent a further communist advance has failed. It has resulted in resentment and a violent upsurge of self-respect. It has produced extraordinary situations. Countries like Yugoslavia and Egypt, which are important for 'strategic' reasons, are able to play the East against the West and secure large financial support from both sides without any advantage being achieved for the cause of democracy. On the contrary the spectacle of aid being poured into such openly totalitarian countries has disheartened those observers who genuinely believe that the West wishes to serve democracy. It has created confusion and weakened the morality of the Western attitude and the ethics of Western economic action.

What is wanted is a pronouncement of Western determination to fight world poverty. The imagination of the world would be instantly captured if the West would initiate a constructive policy giving palpable results, irrespective of any considerations as to the immediate anti-communist or other political advantages to be derived from it. The only guiding conditions of such aid should be the genuine desire to fight poverty for the benefit of the people concerned, and therefore to advance democracy which is the only form of government truly serving the interests of the people. Such a bold approach must have certain characteristics.

In the first place the very idea of 'aid' is repulsive. Aid means unilateral giving. It suggests superiority. There is a giver and a receiver. Such labels must lead to a lowering of national self-esteem in the receiving country. It is, therefore, vitiated from the start. If there still is any doubt in the minds of the Western statesmen about this problem one need only point to the signal

success achieved by the Colombo Plan. Though still compara-
tively small in scale the economic co-operation between the
countries covered by the Colombo Plan has resulted in mutual
respect and friendship. The Western contribution is important,
yet it has no stigma attached to it. It is not 'aid'. It is the contribution made by a wealthier brother to the other members of the
same family, and it is clearly understood by all that the results
obtained are for the good of all. The only objective pursued by
all is the economic development of depressed areas, which cannot
but benefit all parties concerned and particularly the area directly
affected.

'Aid' must be replaced by co-operation. The entire basis of
Western economic action must be changed. Instead of regarding
the recipient countries as helpless politically, in dire need of
economic 'aid' so as to make them capable of resisting communism, they must be treated as part of the great family of Man.
When the Washington Federal Government decided to embark
upon the Tennessee Valley Authority Scheme it did not adopt an
attitude of pontifical superiority towards that particularly depressed area of the United States. That vast enterprise solved
many internal problems of great concern to the whole of the
United States, quite apart from producing an immediate advantage to the inhabitants of the Tennessee Valley. It was in no
way an 'aid'. In order to set their economic action in the right
perspective the Western countries must offer the means to help
solve the problems of poverty for the benefit, not only of the
recipient country, but of the whole world, including the donor
states. The Western world should now put forward an enlightened world population policy, a world health policy, and a world
economic policy.

This could best be achieved by making it incumbent upon a
World Congress of Democracy to decide the use of the limited
resources at the disposal of the world. Surely the best approach

would be to let the representatives assembled at the World Congress of Democracy make the decisions. A working committee on Prosperity, could draw up recommendations giving a list of priorities of areas, needing large-scale projects in the fight against world poverty. The working committee could make concrete proposals. One example will illustrate the point. The problem of the Palestine refugees is one of the most pressing problems in the whole world today. On strict economic grounds it must rank very high in priority and urgency. On political grounds, even higher. On the assumption that this problem is given first priority in the recommendations made by the World Congress of Democracy, it would be for the World Council of Democracy, or whatever permanent organisation were set up, to co-ordinate democratic action, to cope with the problem. An allocation of, say, £50 million could produce within two to three years a remarkable example of Western determination to fight poverty. Western contribution would no longer be 'aid'; it would merely be its enlightened self-interest—a contribution made by one member of the family of nations to another. It would be made available to the depressed area in an impersonal way, through the Council of Democracy and it would serve democracy. All political advantages that might be derived from it would be a by-product reaped in the form of the goodwill, respect and friendship of the people whom such a scheme would benefit. Let there be no doubt that the moment *one* such scheme is brought into operation the attention of the entire world would be arrested and the psychological effect on all other potential recipients would be enormous and cumulative. The 'aid' which is now scattered around the world with no tangible political results, and certainly with no advantage to the democratic West, could be concentrated on creating such well-defined schemes, one by one. It would in fact amount to a concentration of effort. It would be applied, not where the West wishes, but at the point and the area freely chosen by the assembled representatives at the World Congress of Democracy. It would be, in fact, for the recipients themselves, in assembly, to decide where the help should go. It can confidently be predicted that the results of such an action would be little short of spectacular, at far less cost than the present policy of scattering economic help in order to fill the various anti-communist gaps. It would be a token of Western determination to fight poverty with all its power throughout the world. It would permanently remove the charge that Western help is merely given in order to defend the selfish interests of the West, often enough offered to countries who do not feel threatened by the communist advance. It could no longer be associated with the Western military effort to prevent the further spread of communism.

Such schemes should be impressive in themselves and fully justified on economic grounds alone. One can think immediately of a number of economic development schemes in this category which would justify and make the initial outlay pay over the years. The assembled representatives at the World Congress of Democracy could instruct an appropriate Committee on Prosperity to balance the strictly business aspect of any schemes considered with that of the overriding importance of the problem of poverty. In this way an imaginative list of priorities could be drawn up. Thus, before long the whole world would look to the Council of Democracy with respect, friendship and trust.

It is invidious to go into further details. They fall outside the scope of this book. But the work done by such organisations as the U.N.I.C.E.F. and the Colombo Plan suggests the correct lines of approach. It may be of interest to mention that over the 1950–54 period the United Kingdom contributed about $7 million to the programme. Over the same period the United Kingdom drew out of this enlightened, undoubtedly generous contribution $14·5 million in payments to British experts, for transportation, for equipment, etc. In other words the schemes thus embarked upon by the Western powers can be made to pay for themselves in the long run and produce a material reward, as well as a spiritual one, to the donor countries.

Two adjacent aspects of the problem of a world economic policy, as here envisaged, must be mentioned.

The communist world has long had a deliberate trade policy for political ends. It has achieved spectacular results by concentrating on one particular market at a time, outbidding all competition there. This trade policy seems to be directed at this moment mostly on the Middle East, Afghanistan, and, through China, at Nepal. It is evident that whenever the communist powers decide to enter one particular market for political ends they will sell goods and offer services so much below cost that no effective Western economic competition can stand a chance. It is argued that the West, under these circumstances, cannot fight this deliberate communist economic effort. The argument is groundless. The West should embark upon an economic world policy with a view to fighting poverty; all other advantages, and particularly the political advantages, should be only a by-product. If this is firmly born in mind communist competition need not be feared. Suppose that the West decides to fight poverty in one particular area. Suppose that the communist powers decide for political reasons to make an offer to produce the same scheme at a lower cost. The West has two alternatives, either to outbid the communists or to let them carry out the project. Either course of action cannot but benefit the world. Open competition for world prosperity will only be beneficial to the entire world, without a material influence on the balance of power between the two contending political systems. The economic strength of the West is so great and so capable of further expansion, provided such an imaginative world-wide policy is embarked upon, that it will not take long before the communist world, in open competition with the democratic West, would fail to deliver the goods, and leave the field open for Western democracy to give the tangible proof, easily ascertainable by the whole world, of democracy's superiority over communism. Such an open competition seems to be greatly desired by the Soviets at this moment precisely because they expect the West to continue their present, haphazard, un-co-ordinated economic action. If, however, the West embarks upon a long-term economic development scheme, as it is here suggested, the world would provide the West with immense new markets, quite apart from the gradual and general rise in the standard of living throughout the world.

The second aspect of this world economic policy which must be mentioned is trade with communist countries. It is a platitude to say that trade with communist countries presents many difficulties. It is an open secret that the greatest amount of friction among the Western Powers has been created by the several trade policies pursued, at variance with one another. Britain favours trade with China. The United States opposes it. Britain and France favour the release of many of the items now on the embargo list, and trade with the countries of Eastern Europe, and particularly with Eastern Germany and Russia. West Germany has yet to define her trade policy but already has an important trade with Eastern Germany although it pays lip-service to the American attitude. By offering advantages now to one, now to another, of the Western countries, Communist Russia and to a certain extent China have succeeded in creating bad feeling and at times strained relations among the Western democracies.

No Western policy towards communism can hope to be successful without coping effectively with the problem of economic relations with the communist world. It is essential that a perfectly co-ordinated economic policy towards the communist countries should be evolved by the West. This could be done. All countries belonging to such an organisation as the Council of Democracy could conclude trade agreements and agree to trade with the communist world only on the recommendation of the Council of Democracy, which would offer the same opportunities to all democratic member-states without exception. The first result would be the elimination of the bad feeling now created by the benefits which certain countries derive from trading with the communist world, whereas those benefits are denied to the countries who refuse to engage in such trade.

The advantages to be derived from a unitary, well co-ordinated democratic policy, would be immediate, but the possibilities for the future are even more promising. The area of contact and the extent of trade with communist countries could be vastly increased without damage to the Western world. If the West embarks upon a consistent policy of defending and promoting democracy everywhere it could greatly increase its trade with the communist countries without prejudicing its position. At this moment, the motives and the sincerity of Western pronouncements are questioned because often they are at variance with Western economic interests. This the communists well know and skilfully play upon, not only in their propaganda but in the entire conduct of their integrated policy towards the West. For them the economic arm is merely the counterpart and complement of the political arm, both enforcing the same policy. But if the West declares unambiguously its complete opposition to communism and engages in a consistent campaign of denouncing it both in the United Nations Organisation and outside it, and embarks upon a policy of open competition with communism in the economic field throughout the world, then the West need fear nothing from increasing its trade with the communist countries. Trade with the communist countries should not be sought if the productivity of the West finds sufficient markets in the free world. But if it does not it can increase trade with the communist world on a strictly business basis.

The West can and should enter into political negotiations with the communist world for the settlement of any particular conflict on a strict bargaining basis, provided its fundamental opposition to communism is restated without wavering. In the same way, if the profound opposition to communism is made clear, and the policy pursued in the economic field consistent with this opposition, the West can trade with the communist countries without any damage to itself. No one would then accuse the West of having an economic policy blatantly contradicting its avowed political purpose. No one could interpret a trade agreement with some communist country as a change of policy, and trade with the communists would be entered into if thought to be beneficial to the whole democratic position *vis-à-vis* communism. It would be for the Central Planning organs of the democratic world to appraise the situation both from a long as well as a short-term point of view and to recommend appropriate action.

In the absence of such organs for co-ordinating economic policy, the West can make grave mistakes. It is rumoured, for example, that the West intends to make its surplus stocks available below cost to the communist countries. The problem of stocks is an acute one in America and the effect of the disposal of those stocks on the world markets could be dangerous. One need only quote the problem of wheat surpluses, and the enormous amount of bad feeling caused by Britain's attitude towards the International Wheat Agreement, or that of the disposal of $1\frac{1}{2}$ million bales of American cotton surplus stocks.

The establishment of a World Council of Democracy with a permanent secretariat could have a very favourable effect on problems of over-production and raw materials. It could accumulate stocks, if necessary, and then dispose of them below cost to the people of the depressed areas of the world. It would become, in fact, an effective instrument for fighting world poverty. What is here suggested amounts to a scheme comparable to that of food subsidies in the United Kingdom. If bread and milk can be made available to the people of this country below cost, the difference being borne by the taxpayer, there is no reason why it should not be possible for bread and cloth to be made available to the hungry and the naked of the world. It need hardly be added that such action would prove the sincerity of Western purpose beyond any question. It would not merely be a problem of making a wheat loan, like the important one made to India, but actually fighting poverty on a world-wide scale with funds collected from the taxpayer of prosperous countries.

Cultural exchanges between the communists and the democratic world are desirable. The West should come in contact with the cultures of the great Euro-Asian lands even though they are today under communist dictatorship. But cultural exchanges are used by the communists almost exclusively for political purposes. Even such an innocuous event as the Hastings International Chess Congress is used by the Soviet Ambassador, Mr. J. Malik, to further communist propaganda. One may shrink away in horror at the idea of having all activities regulated and rebel when it is suggested that even cultural exchanges between the communists and the democratic West should be carefully sifted and planned. A reaction greatly to be applauded, but the emphasis is wrongly placed.

The West wishes no control over its cultural activity, for no 'regulated' culture is worthy of the name. The West, however must accept the facts of the communist challenge. And the communists are skilfully using the great cultural achievements of the peoples whom they now rule in order to further their political aims. It is essential, therefore, that, before accepting any cultural exchange, its consequences should be carefully considered, not only from a national aspect, but from the point of view of the interests of the whole democratic community of nations. It should be realised, for instance, that the Soviets may attempt, as they have done in the past, to create a particularly favourable climate of opinion in a certain country so as to prepare the ground for some political move. If this is realised the cultural exchanges can take place, even from Soviet initiative, without danger to the Western country concerned and without prejudicing the all-important good relations between the democratic countries of the West.

The important task of carefully considering the advisability of cultural exchanges should be given to the democratic world organisation. The appropriate organ of such an organisation would reject those suggestions of cultural contacts which the communists clearly seek only for the sake of advancing their political purposes; it would greatly encourage all contacts which do not harm the vital interests of the West and it could permit, without any damage to the West, many cultural exchanges specially planned by the communists for political purposes, for the good reason that to be 'forewarned is to be forearmed'.

The need for a co-ordinating agency for the entire democratic world is patent. Ideally, it should have executive powers; obviously not to be achieved before the time is ripe for world government. A consultative status, however, would be enough for the moment. But it would be beneficial to take the whole world as its province. It would have the task of studying the relations of democracy with the rest of the world. It should have the responsibility of recommending the correct line of action. It should give its opinion on all contacts between democracy and communism. In this way ambiguity is avoided, confusion of meaning made impossible and greatly enlarged contacts between East and West feasible because their limited nature would be understood by all. One would no longer word official communiqués at the end of conferences in high-sounding phrases which would proclaim the unity of East and West in their search for peace, when the West envisages genuine peace today and the communists refer to a *communist* world peace after all bourgeois capitalist governments have been destroyed. One would no longer announce the determination of East and West to achieve German unity when the West has in mind a united democratic Germany free to decide its own fate, whereas the communists only visualise a united Germany under communist rule.

Above all real unity among democratic powers could be achieved. The spectacle of a France, pursuing its own direct approach to Moscow, thereby disrupting the democratic 'front', which is so much in the realm of possibility, would no longer darken the horizon. Any new idea as to the policy to be pursued by democracy would first be considered by the democratic powers through their permanent organisation and then turned into reality or rejected by the normal democratic process of discussion and argument. *Vis-à-vis* communism, however, the entire democratic world would have a unitary, perfectly integrated policy. Such a bold and consistent democratic policy would have important consequences on the problem of disarmament itself. Unity of command of all democratic forces could achieve an efficiency and a concentration of effort the like of which the scattered attempts to create security through the present policy could never hope to achieve. The minimum requirements of the democratic countries as a whole for the defence of democracy could be related directly to the communist power in Russia and China. Russia and China should be served notice that any further advance of communism would invite retaliation upon themselves. It is in the interest of the communist powers to maintain large forces only (*a*) if they feel threatened by the West or (*b*) if they consider it possible to use their forces for a further advance of communism. If neither of these circumstances exists it is obvious that maintaining large armed forces, whose effectiveness is only relative in any case, merely saps the economic strength of the country and reduces the economic success of the régime. The contingency under (*a*) above, does not obtain. The Geneva Summit meeting convinced the Soviet leaders that the Western leaders, and particularly Eisenhower, are profoundly peaceful in their intentions. They must maintain large armed forces, therefore, only because they still think that a further advance of communism is possible through the use of armed forces. Such a conclusion can only be drawn by the Soviet leaders precisely because of the confused, contradictory and often impulsive policy which some of the Western partners pursue from time to time. The men in the Kremlin can continue to look forward to a communist advance, arms in hand, only because they can still hope with some justification to divide the West.

If, on the other hand, the unity of the West is made clear to all, through the creation of a permanent world democratic authority on the lines suggested, then the situation would be profoundly altered. The chances of the communists exploiting democratic disunity and using their armed forces for communist conquest would be nil. Under such circumstances it would be in the interest of Russia and China to reduce their armed forces, provided the Western democracies also reduce theirs. Only because of the ambiguous policy now pursued is it possible for the communist powers to keep up the pretence that they wish to live at peace with the rest of the world and yet maintain enormous armed forces, justifying them to the world as their legitimate defence against American designs, but, in reality, hoping to use them for further communist conquest.

XIV

CONCLUSION

THE search for a correct Western policy goes on unabated. It is a healthy sign. 'Let us have faith in ourselves and in our ideals and right will surely triumph,' Sir Winston Churchill urged us when he addressed the Primrose League dinner party at the beginning of 1956.

This is a time when the problems confronting us must be faced in all their reality. The West believes in the defence of democracy. The West, therefore, must abide by the tenets of democracy and fight a clean fight, always open to inspection, which is instinct in the very nature of a functioning democracy.

Today, it is realised that the West has lost the initiative. This is, at any rate, what many Western statesmen tell us. But the truth is far more disturbing than that. The truth is that the West has never had the initiative in its conflict with communism, not even at the time of the Marshall Plan, the boldest and most imaginative of all Western moves since the war. The West has never had the initiative because its entire policy rests on a false assumption and is conducted with antiquated, utterly unsuitable methods, incapable of solving the problems of the modern world. But if the West consciously adopts a constructive, long-term policy of defending and promoting the cause of democracy throughout the world, the West will recover the initiative, never to lose it again, because the cause of democracy is fundamentally right. Democracy will triumph because only through democracy can Man achieve his full stature, only through democracy can he develop the fullness of his qualities and personality, and only through free democratic institutions can he have the right to think and speak freely. If the battle of ideas with communism is imaginatively understood the West need fear nothing. Once the communist challenge is accepted on the solid ground of democracy's own choosing, and fought with the democratic weapons of truth and open debate, then the victory is assured. The West is equipped, by the very nature of the democratic life which it leads, to deal with new situations in a new way. From the free flow of ideas, which is inherent in a democracy, the West will find the right policy to meet any emergency. Democracy works slowly. This is inevitable. But solutions to even the most trying and obstinate of problems are eventually found for, in a democracy, all are called to use their imagination and ability in the service of defending the free life of the community for the enjoyment of all. There is no magic about it. The strength of democracy rests on the most solid foundation of all: the people themselves. And the people are sound. They hate war and abhor cruelty. They hate injustice and reject tyranny.

A great deal has been written about the 'fundamental' changes and the 'democratisation' of Soviet Russia since Stalin's death. Changes undoubtedly have taken place, most of them directly aimed at establishing the claim to power of the present rulers in the Kremlin. The denunciation of the 'personality cult' and of Stalin, and the reversion to the 'Leninist' principle of 'collective leadership' should not, however, obscure the fact that the present 'collective' leaders of communism are strictly applying the technique for capturing power and the method of government by force which were evolved under Lenin and Stalin and which are ideally suited for the conquest of a world divided into countless small units, the national states of today. This is the reason why Soviet diplomacy at government level, and Soviet policy aimed at the people, have always opposed any attempt on the part of the non-communist world to unite in any shape or form. The duty of the West today is not merely to bring about a measure of integration and international co-operation in this or that area of the world. The West is called upon to gather together all those forces which are ready and capable of serving, and if necessary of fighting for, democracy. If the West succeeds in gathering the democratic forces in one united fold, it will have created a new situation for which the communists are no longer equipped.

There is no time for complacency. The West must reconsider its entire policy *now*, for the challenge has been made and democracy is now losing ground everywhere in the uncommitted world. The present situation is so dangerous that there is no single country in the uncommitted world where democracy and the friends of democracy are not on the defensive, attacked at every turn by the disruptive forces which communism aids and abets. In the body politic of the Western world itself there are important communist forces pledged to destroy the free institutions and replace them with those fashioned in the Moscovite forge. Their success at general elections can only be explained by the failure of the democratic forces, which, though they may understand and reject the communist alternative, are not capable of giving an inspiring and consistent lead to the world. Let the West devise an organisation which will achieve unity and give a clear direction for the future.

The world is at a crossing of the ways. The awakened millions, and the millions still to be awakened, are rightly clamouring, or will be clamouring tomorrow, for their place in the sun. This tremendous force, now inclining to see communism as its friend, can be saved from a fatal danger, which will not only spell their own servitude but will also endanger the democratic West and the very existence of the idea of freedom. They must be prevented from choosing the communist road, not by force, cajolery, or guile, but by presenting them with a much more appealing alternative, an alternative which will serve their own best interests as well as the interests of the West.

Let the West make its position clear and carry a simple message into the far corners of the earth.

We are for *Peace*, not only in the West, but everywhere. We are strong, but will not have recourse to war unless war is waged on us or on any of our friends. Your independence, wherever you may be, is of deep concern to us. If you are threatened, you can count on our immediate and unlimited help. We seek no aggrandisement. The moment the emergency is past we shall leave you to manage your own affairs in your own way.

We are for *liberty*. We believe that the best way to achieve liberty is through the free institutions which democracy has brought into being. We are strong because democracy, which is by far the best form of government yet devised on earth, has made us so. You too can be strong by taking the road to democracy. But the decision is yours. We stand by you, ready to share with you our experience and knowledge. But it is for you to devise the exact nature of your own free institutions which will serve your own best interests. Democracy is not a doctrine rigidly to be imposed before it can produce results. Democracy is a way of life which secures the right to live a full life to every member of the community. We rely on all the people who give us their freely chosen support. We do not resort to mass frenzy, fanfares and uniforms, for our strength is derived from the individual. Democracy is the individual choice of every man, who, in the quietness of his soul, knows that only in democracy are his rights fully recognised, against any power on earth. We advocate democracy for you because we know that a world united in democracy is a world united in peace. Never in the history of mankind has democracy wilfully started a war, as the people do not want war. Only democracy, of all forms of government, always acts by the will of the people. If you take the road to democracy you do not have to change your pattern of life, nor your traditions. They receive greater substance and a far better chance of being freely expressed. In a democracy all viewpoints have an equal right to be expressed and are equally entitled to seek general adoption. Democracy merely ensures that the conflicting points of view should struggle for supremacy in an orderly, non-violent fashion. Democracy is agreeing to disagree. It is based on mutual respect. It is a set of rules which assure civilised conduct in society. We believe in democracy and shall defend it against all comers, and are ready to help democrats everywhere. We are firmly on the side of all people in their quest for freedom. We challenge tyranny in all its forms. We denounce dictatorships of the Right as well as the Left. We fought two great wars to defend liberty and stood alone against tyranny when the dictatorship of the Left, which now brandishes the olive branch and releases the dove of peace, stood by and shared in the spoils of the late apocalyptic tyrant. Today, we oppose this dictatorship of the Left, as we yesterday opposed the dictatorships of the Right, because all dictatorships, whatever their guise, destroy the independent will of the individual. We demand of this dictatorship of the Left to release its subject peoples. We condemn it before the tribunal of world opinion as a wicked travesty of high-sounding principles which are belied by the millions of unfortunate fellow men deprived of their individual freedom, now frequently labouring under appalling conditions, in concentration and slave-labour camps. We invite inspection into every aspect of our national life. We challenge the dictatorships of the Left, as we have challenged those of the Right to permit inspection of their forced labour camps by the representatives of the uncommitted nations.

We stand for *prosperity*, not only in our own countries, but throughout the world. We invite you to work with us and help us select those areas where it is best to apply our resources, so as to contribute to the general material advancement of the world. We shall fight poverty throughout the world with all our might and we shall willingly accept sacrifices in our own standard of living, in order to eliminate dire poverty from the face of the earth. We consider our contribution to be our duty towards the family of Man, of which we are part.

We are for *peace*; we are for *liberty*; we are for *prosperity*.

This is a message which the world will understand. But it is not enough merely to proclaim it, as it has in part been proclaimed from the Atlantic Charter onwards, to the Point Four Programme and the Washington Declaration. The West must accept its full implications. The West must give performance, and a startling performance it must be. Above all, the West must find a new consistent policy which will restore confidence in the sincerity of Western purpose.

The vista of human endeavour and achievement, on a worldwide basis, is truly tremendous, particularly now at the dawn of the nuclear age. Untold development, for the benefit of the entire mankind, is for the West to bring about. The best of the new generation of the West are already searching for a new purpose, for purposelessness and inhumanism, as exemplified by the all-powerful state, seem to be the toils from which they want to escape. Could there be a higher purpose than to serve mankind, the *whole* of mankind? The religious will do justice in the sight of God by serving his fellow men. The humanist could not wish for a better outlet for his energy and talent. Let the leaders of the democratic West re-define their position and adopt a policy at once unyielding yet flexible, strong yet mellow and malleable, determined yet practical: a policy which will enlist the freely given allegiance of the best sons of all nations, regardless of race or creed, an allegiance given in the service of humanity as a whole.

The sands of time are running out. Hesitation, parochialism and self-interest will lead inevitably to the loss of one position after another. And the effort which, today, would turn the tide against the ever-advancing forces of materialism, will have to be made a thousand-fold tomorrow when the West will be locked in a life-or-death struggle with tyranny, the outcome of which no one should dare predict.

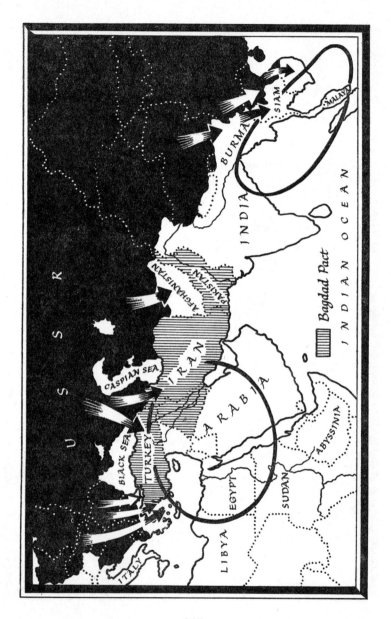

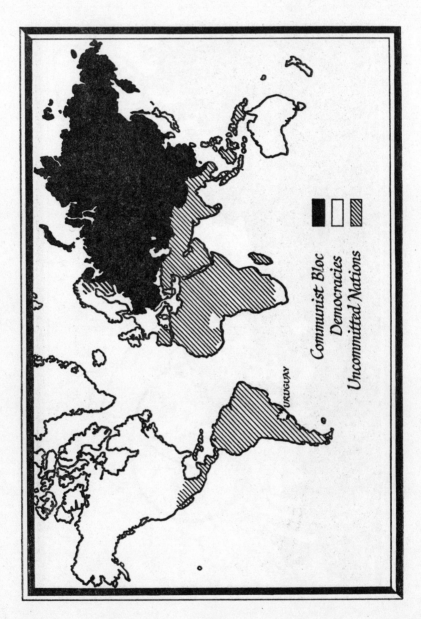

Communist Bloc
Democracies
Uncommitted Nations

URUGUAY